MW00325078

Healing God's People

Theological and Pastoral Approaches

A Reconciliation Reader

Edited by
THOMAS A. KANE, CSP

Paulist Press
New York / Mahwah, NJ

Cover image by Kirill Kurashov / Shutterstock.com
Cover design by Sharyn Banks
Book design by Lynn Else

Library of Congress Cataloging-in-Publication Data

Healing God's people : theological and pastoral approaches : a reconciliation reader / edited by Thomas A. Kane, CSP.
    pages cm
    ISBN 978-0-8091-4822-6 (alk. paper) — ISBN 978-1-58768-230-8
    1. Reconciliation—Religious aspects—Christianity. 2. Reconciliation—Religious aspects—Catholic Church. I. Kane, Thomas A., 1945– editor of compilation.
    BT738.27.H43 2013
    234'.5—dc23

                                                            2012046218

ISBN: 978-0-8091-4822-6 (Paperback)
ISBN: 978-1-58768-230-8 (E-Book)

Published by Paulist Press
997 Macarthur Boulevard
Mahwah, New Jersey 07430

www.paulistpress.com

Printed and bound in the United States of America

In loving memory of
James J. Young, CSP,
friend and mentor,
who taught me to reach out
to the lost and brokenhearted
with love and compassion.

Prayer for Reconciliation

God of compassion,
You sent Jesus to proclaim a time of mercy
reaching out to those who had no voice,
releasing those trapped by their own shame,
and welcoming those scorned by society.

Make us ambassadors of reconciliation.
Open our ears that we may listen
with respect and understanding.
Touch our lips that we may speak
your words of peace and forgiveness.
Warm our hearts that we may bring
wholeness to the broken-hearted and
dissolve the barriers of division.

Guide the work of your Church
and renew us with the Spirit of your love.
Help us and all people shape a world
where all will have a place,
where the flames of hatred are quenched,
and where all can grow together as one.

Forgive, restore and strengthen us through
our Lord Jesus Christ. Amen.

CONTENTS

Contents

FOREWORD

As Christians reflect on reconciliation, I am regularly drawn to St. Paul's observation in 2 Corinthians 5:16–17: "From now on, therefore, we regard no one from a human point of view....If anyone is in Christ, there is a new creation: everything old has passed away; see, everything has become new!" But I have, for many years, been provocatively attracted to another translation, equally accurate from the Greek: "If anyone is in Christ, there is a whole new world."And to this, we'll return frequently, for I believe, it is the vantage of the "new world" that frames our work for reconciliation.

In May 2010, I returned to the United States after eleven years living and working in Israel/Palestine. On the seam between Jerusalem and Bethlehem, I was the rector at the Ecumenical Institute for Theological Studies at Tantur. The institute sits on a hill, often serving as an "oasis of sound discourse." To Tantur, many professional reconcilers came to try out their methods, to see if they might bring the Israelis and the Palestinians together to bring about peace. For many in the peacemaking business, it's the Holy Grail of all disputes to reconcile. We, at Tantur, were privileged to be neutral—but not indifferent—onlookers to these intense, heartfelt efforts. My thoughts in this short foreword reflect some of what I learned from those sessions.

But now, I am back in the United States, or, as I quip, "from the Holy Land to the Promised Land!" After eleven years in Jerusalem, I can hardly claim to have returned victorious in bringing peace to the land. But I have returned humbler and less credulous that dialogue, by itself, can cast a kind of magic spell on those who take part. Simply putting two adversaries in the room to talk seldom brings about reconciliation. No, I have come back much more sober about the relative ease with which any kind of reconciliation can occur.

Closely allied with the process of reconciliation is the phenomenon of forgiveness. Even before leaving the United States in 1999, I trembled each time the lectionary brought me to preach about forgiveness. One Jewish commentator on Jesus claimed that, while forgiveness is found abundantly in Jewish religious life, in Jesus' preaching, he brought forgiveness to a centrality that far surpassed that which he found in his own religious worldview. So we Christian preachers must address the centrality and obligation to forgive with unrelenting regularity. It can become easy, too easy. We domesticate passages like "Turn the other cheek" from being an outrageous and demanding call to an easily applied bit of advice. Easily offered advice is easily ignored. No, forgiveness is complicated, multilayered, and part of larger life-processes.

So I left Jerusalem, even as I had arrived there, with wariness about the ease of forgiveness and reconciliation. But I also showed up with a keen interest in and fascination for reconciliation and how it might play itself out in Israel/Palestine. Here, I share some of the lessons I learned there in the Holy Land as a foreword to this collection of essays on reconciliation.

As rector of the Tantur Ecumenical Institute, international facilitators often approached me to help them find subjects for their very carefully plotted reconciliation programs: "Could you please help us in getting ten Palestinians and ten Israelis for our workshop at Tantur?" "Well, I'll do the best I can, but first tell me, which language would you like them to speak? Arabic, Hebrew, or, maybe English?" "Well, English, of course. We don't know Arabic or Hebrew."

Can one imagine German project directors coming to the United States to address our issues with race relations, asking for ten African Americans, ten Latinos, and ten Euro Americans…and,

"By the way, please make sure that they all speak German…that's the only language we know"? Do we know the language of those who need reconciliation? Can we afford a translator? Can we afford *not to have* a translator?

That was one of my first lessons: sometimes we do not *know the language* of those who need reconciliation; we only know our own language.

"If anyone is in Christ, there is a whole new world…."

Another time, I was approached by an American sister who wished to come to Tantur for one of our continuing education programs. She asked, "Do you accept Catholic feminists?" I replied, "Of course, we welcome all who come in good faith." But I went on to caution her that sometimes our own cultural biases—however virtuous we deem them—get in the way rather than facilitate understanding and dialogue. I suggested that if by being a Catholic feminist, she had already judged that veiled women were wearing symbols of their own subjection and inferiority, then maybe there would be a problem.[1] I invited her to come without preconceptions (of course, who can do that completely?) and to *listen to the experience* of those women who are Muslim and who wear a *hijab*. Not so easy.

"If anyone is in Christ, there is a whole new world…."

What are the tools that the locals use for reconciliation? In some more rural Arab areas of Palestine, one may find a community's use of a *muhtar*, a wise elder, for reconciliation. That is, when two individuals or families are in dispute, they hand over their case to the *muhtar*, who makes a judgment and that judgment is final. He assesses the facts of the case, determines who is right, and sometimes even imposes a penalty on the one who has brought an unjust charge. Such penalties discourage, many times, frivolous or fraudulent cases.[2] At any rate, what I learned is that reconciliation may have local expressions far different from our Western customs and from which we may have something to learn.

One may have the impression that what has been said so far reflects negatively on international professional reconciliation projects. Actually, I came to admire those who gave their lives to peacemaking, even as I reserved some skepticism. But I also learned much from their earnest enthusiasm. All had something to teach me. Indeed, I was significantly impressed by one reconciliation project: the "Compassionate Listening Project" (CLP) out of Seattle, Washington.[3] While many of us feel that we already have fine listening skills, for many still, a pause in conversation is the time to "reload." The CLP facilitators who came to Tantur taught the gathered Christians, Muslims, and Jews rather that listening begins with the heartfelt feeling that "I really want to hear your experience." That, to me, became the bedrock for any effective effort at reconciliation.

So the question the CLP facilitators lay before all of us is, "Who are being reconciled, how do we see them?" Do we consider them people desperate for what we have to offer? Or, do we come with a love for the bungling, the strong, the heroic, the incompetent, the unworthy, and yes, the sinful, people? I saw this need for a genuine caring for the other in abundance in the Arab-Israeli conflict.

As many of you know, part of my living out the Paulist mission has been to work for reconciliation between Jewish and Christians. Ever since those days more than thirty-five years ago when I wrote a thesis, partially provoked by studying how Christians have treated and taught about Jews over the millennia, I have worked more or less intensely on improving relations between Christians and Jews. So the long-haul work for reconciliation has been part of my life story. At the same time, the longer I have been at it, in various venues, the more difficult I understand it to be. Here is one place where practice does *not necessarily make* perfect.

The longer I've worked, the more I've come to conclude that true reconciliation comes only with the empathy for the other.

When I left Jerusalem in 2010, I heard a story of a departure similar to mine. In 2001, Monsignor Richard Mathes, a German Catholic priest, was leaving the country after many years of service at the Notre Dame of Jerusalem Center. At his farewell, he said, "When I first came to Jerusalem many years ago, for the first five years, I was sympathetic to the Jews and angry at the Palestinians. During my second five years, as I saw what Israelis do on a regular and systematic way to the Palestinians, I was angry with the Jews and sympathetic to the Palestinians. Now, in these last five years, my heart breaks for both of them."

While Msgr. Mathes obviously paints with broad strokes, his words also point to a reality that I wish to underscore here. And that is, part of the hard work of reconciliation is getting to know *and care for* the persons who may or may not wish to reconcile. To get to know them means, at least, to know their experience, their narrative, their feelings about their narrative, and their access to power in the relationship. How many times have we heard someone justify himself with the words, "Some of my best friends are Jews"? These words often cloak an excuse for antisemitic behavior or attitudes. But what if *none* of my friends are Jews? What if I have never met an Arab? How do I see them as human beings, with individual stories and personal aspirations to raise their children in peace and prosperity? Getting to know and share the aspirations of the other is often the condition for successful reconciliation.

An Israeli rabbi helped me to learn this profound lesson. He told me of his experience in a Palestinian-Israeli dialogue like the ones that frequently occurred at Tantur. Although the face-to-face encounter was conducted in English, both sides spoke quickly and vigorously about their experience and all the terrible things that the other had done to them. At one point in the screaming match, a Palestinian citizen of Israel shouted that, in the weeks following the 1948 war, Jewish Israelis had destroyed more than four hundred Galilee villages. My friend, as he candidly told me, at first brushed off this outrageous claim as one more example of Palestinian propaganda, put forth to cast the Arabs as victims and to invent the Israelis as the powerful, brutal force intent on destroying the Arabs—the usual stuff of propaganda. But my friend decided to look into the history a bit more carefully, beyond what he had been taught in his Jewish day school and his early years in Israel after he had made *aliya* (Jewish immigration into Israel). Consulting only texts he trusted (those written by fellow Jews), my friend found out that, indeed, more than four hundred Arab (many of them Christian) villages had been destroyed in the Galilee *after* the 1948 war. From that moment on, my friend decided that perhaps we are all too susceptible to knowing only one side of multifaceted stories. That is, not everything that my side has told me is true, and not everything that the other side says is a lie.

"If anyone is in Christ, there is a whole new world...."

During the early, very dark days of the Second Intifada (2000–2003), two fatalities profoundly affected all on both sides. Regular reports of arrests, suicide bombs, land confiscation, and checkpoint detentions killed two irreplaceable energies: empathy and hope. But against the apparent loss of empathy and hope, many peacemakers worked on. Those reconcilers I knew and admired most in Israel/Palestine were certainly not all Christian (e.g., my Israeli rabbi friend); indeed most of them were not. They were Jews, Muslims, secularists, and a few Christians, who had been graced by a generosity of spirit that propelled them to work for peace and reconciliation because they saw in "the other"—whether Israeli or Palestinian—something irreducibly valuable. This they did even against the utter darkness of the Second Intifada. To them, I am profoundly grateful for teaching me so much.

And so, what have I learned (and need to keep relearning) after eleven years in one of the world's laboratories of reconciliation?

- The importance of determining what language—literal and figurative—those who take part are using;
- The importance of listening to the experience of the other, especially where there is a significant cultural divide;

- The importance of exploring local, indigenous rituals and tools of reconciliation. Not only have different cultures developed various rituals of reconciliation, they may have something to teach us;
- The importance of listening and wanting to listen to the other;
- The irreplaceable centrality of empathy—feeling with the pain of the other—in reconciliation ministry; and
- The importance of hearing both (or many) sides of the story.

But I wish to add: *in addition to our experience, we Christians must draw on our faith.* With Paul, we believe that "if anyone is in Christ, there is a whole new world." That is, our Christian faith not only strengthens us, but also it gives us a perspective, a viewpoint, and, yes, a bias. For faith is not a matter of seeing different things from what other people see—our faith does not sugarcoat tragic human suffering into something it is not. Rather our faith beckons us to look upon human fracturedness as opportunities for us to be God's instruments in working towards God's kingdom. So the Christian reconciler's gift is to bring a vision in addition to the talents and tools that modern social sciences have developed. Indeed, all have so much to learn from the sociology, anthropology, and psychology, as I learned at Tantur. But our faith fills us with the conviction that those who are to be reconciled are loved by God and, therefore, are objects of our love as well. When the participants at Tantur were gathered by their religious (and not by their national or ethnic) identity, frequently Jews, Muslims, and Christians noted their common affirmation that human beings are made in the image and likeness of God. What a marvelous place to start!

So we have in our hands this superb volume of essays on seeking reconciliation. My experience, certainly not as exhaustive or as scholarly as most of these contributors', leads me to welcome them wholeheartedly. Many of them confirm, with different words and insights, my own experience; others open up new perspectives; and still others challenge my experience—which is precisely what an excellent set of essays should do. Confirm our experience, add to our experience, challenge our experience, and expand our experience. With God's grace, neither empathy nor hope will die in us, and these essays provide some of the inspiration to make sure that does not happen.

Michael McGarry, CSP
President, The Paulist Fathers

Notes

1. The veil or *hijab* is the head covering typical for many Muslim women.

2. Obviously, I am oversimplifying a more complicated process. See George E. Irani and Nathan C. Funk, "Rituals of Reconciliation: Arab-Islamic Perspectives," *Kroc Institute Occasional Paper* #19:OP:2 (2000).

3. See http://www.compassionatelistening.org.

INTRODUCTION

The need for reconciliation and healing is greater now than ever. Divisions within the Church and society seem to grow wider every day, with extremes on all sides. This reader aims to explore the broad landscape of reconciliation and healing from a variety of theological and pastoral viewpoints. The articles and insights of this volume come from my work with the Paulist Fathers' Office of Reconciliation Ministries in Washington, DC, and from two conferences hosted at the Boston College School of Theology and Ministry: *The Road to Reconciliation* (April 2009) and *Healing God's People* (April 2011). While certainly not exhaustive, I hope this volume will introduce the reader to the complexity of the issues and suggest pathways toward developing appropriate pastoral responses. By assisting the Church to call people to conversion and seek healing, we are harbingers of God's mercy as we gather the broken into God's wholeness.

Shawn Copeland opens the volume with a call for hope to meet the challenges of today's Church through the exercise of prophetic ministry. Millions of Catholics, many of them young adults, do not practice their faith and abstain from the table of Jesus Christ. At the same time, the church in the United States has also experienced a major crisis of moral authority through the scandal of abusive clergy and a lack of transparency within the leadership. In addition, gender and sexual issues—especially in the areas around priesthood, abortion, and sexuality—are not easily addressed pastorally. Some claim that the Church is out of touch with the culture around it, as the impulse toward secularity drives popular culture into forms and laws that seem ever more distant from some church teaching.

Reconciliation is a lifelong process, not an end result that one can achieve easily, once and for all. It operates on many levels: the personal, the social-communitarian, the national, and the international, requiring a depth of pastoral skill sets. Robert Schreiter takes us on a journey along these various paths and presents a theological roadmap for this ministry. Thomas Stegman gives us the biblical foundations; while Ray Helmick explores the building blocks of forgiveness. Thomas Porter examines the practice of restorative justice and presents a new model of table fellowship. Reconciliation continues to point to a process of deeper union with God and the people of the Church, and ultimately, with all women and men on earth.

Kate Dooley examines the sacramental side of reconciliation. The use, or disuse, of the sacrament of reconciliation might symbolize the disarray that the Church is experiencing at times. While the Church speaks of compassion and mercy, it focuses primarily on one celebration of a sacramental process that has become difficult for many believers. The sacrament, rather than being a ready point of access, appears to many as a roadblock. Peter Fink suggests creative, alternative sacramental approaches.

There are also stumbling blocks for many people with the way the Church sometimes responds to sensitive issues. So it is not only people who need to be reconciled, but the Church itself must engage in the process of becoming reconciled to both its own members and the greater society. While maintaining the integrity of its doctrine, this work will require an open and welcoming spirit.

When Jesus taught us to pray, he insisted that we offer forgiveness as we have experienced it. This is particularly true today as we examine our global approach to people in crisis and our relationship with other church communities. Thomas Ryan and Rodney Petersen take a fresh look at reconciliation from an ecumenical and an interfaith perspective.

On the practical side, reconciliation ministry requires compassion and cultural sensitivity. Frank Desiderio, Melissa Kelley, and Hosffman Ospino explore these pastoral realms. As a church, we need to recommit ourselves to a ministry of forgiveness and healing so that the laity within the church will become ambassadors of reconciliation. The process will primarily be one of dialogue, listening, sharing, and renewing contacts across all levels of Church life. The process is multi-leveled, with invitations to the wider society, to the wider church, to parish communities, and to individual Catholics, whatever their pastoral situation might be. United in one mission, we must all be about the business of reconciliation.

Francine Cardman returns to the theme of hope and its everyday practices that enable us to persevere in the work of reconciliation. Hope is the firm conviction that all of creation is interconnected. A reconciling community knows its dependence on God and its interdependence on one another, a community of shared need, shared dignity, and shared hope. The process depends on the Holy Spirit, whose love seals the union of Father and Son, and is the bond by which all recognize themselves as brothers and sisters, united and connected, healed and still in need of healing.

Many thanks to all the authors who contributed to this volume and who dedicate their lives to the work of healing; to Melinda Brown-Donovan at Boston College; to the Board members of Paulist Reconciliation Ministries; and to Paulist Fathers who continue to welcome all searchers back to the table of the Lord.

Thomas A. Kane, CSP
Editor

I
PRELUDE

THE CHURCH'S PROPHETIC CHALLENGE

M. Shawn Copeland

The contemporary context of global living is compound-complex
and precarious at every level—biological and psychological, political and economic, cultural, religious, and intellectual. We know
the facts: Scientists repeatedly warn us about the damage our style
of life does to our planetary ecosystem, and these injuries, in turn,
contribute to changes in temperature of the oceans, the spread of
drought and deserts, and the reduction of harvests. These atmo-
spheric and geographic shifts trigger food insecurity, hunger, and
malnutrition. In the past five years alone, floods, hurricanes, wild
fires, tsunamis, earthquakes, and volcanic eruptions have increased
in frequency and ferocity in various regions of the planet, anni-
hilating human populations, devastating animal and plant life,
and destroying infrastructure. Poverty and war remain the twin
scourges of our world and the principal causes of hunger. Roughly
982 million people live each day on $1.00 or less. Armed conflict
spawns the proliferation of refugee camps as brutality and rape
drive people from their homes, villages, and towns. The persistence of HIV/AIDS along with ballooning incidences of polio and
tuberculosis has reawakened old plagues in new places.[1] In both
Russian and U.S. prisons, more and more women and men fall
prey to multidrug-resistant tuberculosis.[2] Large numbers of children, women, and men endure violence to their reputations, persons, and lives because of homophobia, misogyny and sexism,

3

antisemitism, and racism, including anti-immigrant bias. Uncritical affirmation of the liberal market's vulgarization of individuality as license has led to exploitation of the poor and the manipulation and commercialization of desire. Staggered by the fragility of the global economy, we have begun to glimpse just how gravely empty, tasteless market culture has jeopardized and undermined our capacity for being human and for authentic spirituality.[3] Our culture, in its reflective or contemplative mode, is collapsing underneath the weight of kitsch, which has eviscerated the moral and spiritual content. We are amusing ourselves to death.[4] At the same time, in the past decade, as an *institution*, the Church has initiated a perplexing reassessment of the meaning of the Second Vatican Council; as *Mystery*, the Church is undergoing waves of shattering agony provoked by abuse of persons and authority; as *pilgrim people of God*, the Church edges toward sacramental famine.

The cumulative evidence is glaring: On almost every level, both as individuals and as a community, we feel powerless. On a cultural level, we feel bewildered and estranged by the rapidity of fads and shifts in values. On a social level, we feel vulnerable to the power of our technologies. On an intellectual level, we feel overwhelmed by the amount and intricacy of information required to make good moral and ethical choices. On a religious level, we feel betrayed and ignored by our pastoral leaders, who daily contend with multiple competing and, often, conflicting demands, and who themselves often feel betrayed and ignored.

"A prophetic ministry is imperative," Walter Brueggemann argues, "when a situation is so new and different that the old traditions no longer supply clear guidance and adequate motivation for facing history responsibly."[5] My summary of our contemporary social, cultural, and religious context supports the claim that we need a prophetic ministry to rightly discern our situation and our freedom. Any Christian understanding of prophecy or prophetic ministry must be rooted in prophecy as it developed in ancient Israel.

The Hebrew prophets were women and men, who were chosen and called by God to speak or enact a word given to them by God for the life and future of God's people. The prophets were invested with a critical public function, and the prophet's ability to read the "signs of the times" was indispensable for the people's relationship with God. Prophets bear witness, testify to what they see, and stand up and against whatever avoids or violates the demands of the covenantal relationship. The prophet's task was not one of prediction, for truth-events may never be manufactured and divine power can never be subordinated to magic; nor was the prophet's task one of proclaiming immutable decrees. The prophets were signposts sent by God to orient the people to their freedom and the possibilities of its realization.

The prophet's task, Martin Buber explains, "involves a question, a summons to decision."[6] The true prophet "sets the audience before the choice,"[7] *not the choice before the audience.* When the prophet summons the people before the message of God, the future is not something already fixed or concluded. The future depends upon the people's real decision, their choice in freedom.[8] Thus the prophet witnesses to hope—hope in the people's relationship with God and with one another, hope in the people's disposition before their freedom. And, as Leon Feuer observes, for Israel and its prophets, "Hope was not so much a heavenly gift as a divine requirement."[9]

A Praxis of Hope

With the phrase "praxis of hope," I refer to the dynamic cluster of attitudes, choices, and habits that flows from a more or less steady response to the Christian call to conversion, that seeks prayerful solitude and communal engagement, that shoulders responsibility for the "least" of Jesus' family (Matt 25:37–40), that struggles against all forms of fatalism and yearns in eager obedience for the coming reign of God. Such a praxis is, at once, the cradle and sign of prophetic ministry in the church. Having named the ingredients of a praxis of hope, I now want to transpose some themes Walter Brueggemann has developed into characteristics of hope-filled prophetic ministry. There are five of these:

1. *Personal and private prayer, but never privatized faith, characterizes the life of those called to prophetic ministry.* Without fidelity to a life of prayer, the words spoken are hollow, living shallow, and the capacity for discernment diverted. The exercise of prophetic ministry demands an integrity, which requires those called to be living signs of "God's investment in the history of [God's] people."[10]

2. *Prophetic ministry protests idolatry and ideology.*[11] On the one hand, prophetic ministry uncovers and denounces those idols, which dare to disguise themselves as divine or which dare to handle God mechanistically. On the other hand, because the attempt "to pass" as or "to master" divinity requires an ideology that obscures or intimidates, prophetic ministry exposes and protests half-truths wherever they are found.[12] Thus prophetic ministry is critically alert to the world in which we live, discerns the signs of the times, and uncovers what is *not* of God—what is idolatrous, what attempts to usurp God's place in our lives and in our world. *God must be God*—no nation, no political party, no social class, no gender, no race, no particular ministry, no theology, no church is God. *God must be God.* Ideology critique accompanies the unmasking of idols. Thus, under the tutelage of the Spirit, prophetic ministry turns the spotlight on oppressive structures or institutions, delineates their implications, and uncovers those uncritical assumptions, which allow these structures to appear *natural*, logical, necessary, and permanent.

3. *Prophetic ministry reads the signs of the times, uncovers, and meets hidden and neglected human suffering.* Because social oppression tampers with key values and meanings to insinuate ideological interpretations

of the culture, the challenge of reading the signs of the times is a most difficult task. Prophetic ministry takes responsibility for this reading. It demystifies social oppression, naming the intentional distortions and manipulations of the cultural and social orders to the advantage of those who are privileged and to the disadvantage of those who are excluded and despised.[13] In our own U.S. situation, prophetic ministry confronts our calculated abuse of the poor and homeless, protests our animosity and violence toward immigrant peoples, in particular, Hispanic/Latinos, questions our deliberate neglect and denial of African Americans, rejects our betrayal and abandonment of the cities, repudiates our continued marginalization of the indigenous peoples, and denounces our staggering disregard for the millions whom our penal system incarcerates. Prophetic ministry calls us *as* church to the demands of ethical living, to act concretely for justice in the here-and-now for the sake of the gospel.

4. *Prophetic ministry maintains an open and questioning posture toward all established power.* Through coercion, corruption, or seduction, all the various forms of established power seek legitimation and hegemony. They come with glittering offers of security and success or with threats and intimidation. In return, they urge us to lower our vision, restrict our horizon, and cling to the immediate. But what is on offer aims to compromise our openness and bind our freedom.

   Prophetic ministry contests any abuse of power. While acknowledging "power matters enormously," prophetic ministry adamantly insists "power does not matter ultimately."[14] Prophetic ministry repudiates any domestication of the message of the Gospel, any repressive limitation on human agency in the historical process of our salvation. It witnesses to church and society that God is the *locus* of human hope. Thus, prophetic ministry stands critically

7

attentive and responsive to, but independent of, present circumstances. It helps us to understand that God does not absolutize the present; thus, we should be wary of taking the present with "excessive seriousness."[15] The future God desires for us, the plans God has in mind for us for a future full of hope (Jer 29:11), relativizes the present that we may have come to overvalue. God, in God's own unqualified and unrestricted freedom, will gift us with a future that we cannot imagine. For God has staked the gift of that future, indeed, the future of divine life in us, in our openness to the divine and to the human.

5. *Prophetic ministry is an act of unyielding hope that resists despair.*[16] Paulo Freire regards hope as "an ontological need."[17] In other words, we cannot live without hope, we cannot be human without hope, nor without hope shall we drink wine with Jesus in the household of God as he promised (Luke 22:18). Prophetic ministry sets us before our freedom and offers us an account of hope that expands all our "perceived horizons of possibility, broadening our landscape of reality in such a way as to set our present circumstances in a wider perspective and thereby to rob it of its absoluteness."[18] Such an account of hope liberates and invigorates, "transfigures every empirical present by relating" it to God's vision of the future.[19]

These characteristics suggest "a capacity for living in time,"[20] while looking toward the eschatological gift of God's future. They point toward a way of orienting ourselves as *people of hope.*

Notes

1. http://www.care.org/campaigns/hiv,asp?source=170740 250000&channel=default.

2. Paul Farmer, *Pathologies of Power: Health, Human Rights, and the New War on the Poor* (Berkeley and Los Angeles: University of California Press, 2005), 131.

3. See Gary Dorrien on integrating democratic values into the economic order: Union Theological Seminary, "An Alternative Model: Economic Democracy," You Tube, http://www.youtube.com/watch?v=2F-DmmKKfPY (uploaded March 27, 2009).

4. Morris Berman, *The Twilight of American Culture* (New York: W. W. Norton, 2000), 19; Neil Postman, *Amusing Ourselves to Death: Public Discourse in the Age of Show Business* (New York: Penguin Books, 1986).

5. Walter Brueggemann, *Tradition for Crisis* (Atlanta: John Knox Press, 1968), 129.

6. Martin Buber, *The Prophetic Faith* (New York: Harper & Row, 1949), 104.

7. Ibid., 103, 2–3.

8. Ibid., 2–3.

9. Cited in Leon I. Feuer, "Prophetic Religion in an Age of Revolution," in *Interpreting the Prophetic Tradition: The Goldenson Lectures, 1955–1966* (New York: KTAV Publishing House, Inc., 1969), 182.

10. Ibid.

11. Walter Brueggemann, *Like Fire in the Bones: Listening for the Prophetic Word in Jeremiah* (Minneapolis: Fortress Press, 2006), 79–81.

12. My use of the term *ideology* is pejorative, *not* neutral in the way in which one might say "my ideology." My use is compatible with Lonergan's notion of *bias*, that is, the more or less conscious and intentional decision to refuse corrective insights and to live with distorted understanding and, therefore, to behave and to act in distorted ways in everyday life, see *Collected Works of Bernard Lonergan*, vol. 3, *Insight, A Study of Human Understanding*, 5th ed. (1957; Toronto: University of Toronto Press, 1988), chap. 6–7.

13. In *Justice and the Politics of Difference* (Princeton: Princeton University Press, 1990), political theorist Iris Marion Young argues that social oppression may be found in Western liberal societies through economic exploitation, marginalization, powerlessness, cultural imperialism, and violence. These are "systemic constraints" placed on certain individuals and groups, not by the will of a tyrant, but by the choices and policies made by or on behalf of the privileged few (see page 41).

14. Brueggemann, *Like Fire in the Bones*, 80.

15. Ibid.

16. Ibid., 81.

17. Paulo Freire, *Pedagogy of Hope* (1992; London & New York: Continuum, 1994), 3.

18. Richard Bauckham and Trevor Hart, "The Shape of Time," in *The Future as God's Gift: Explorations in Christian Eschatology*, ed. David Fergusson and Marcel Sarot (Edinburgh: T & T Clark, 2000), 61.

19. Ibid.

20. Glenn Tinder, *The Fabric of Hope: An Essay* (Atlanta: Scholars Press, 1999), 149.

II
THEOLOGIES OF RECONCILIATION

2

ROADS TO RECONCILIATION

Robert J. Schreiter, CPPS

Introduction

Three commemorations were held in 2009 that made the theme of the symposium, "Roads to Reconciliation," especially timely. In November of that year, it was twenty years since the fall of the Berlin Wall—an event emblematic of the collapse of communism in Europe. It was perhaps this event more than anything else that set off a renewed and intense interest in reconciliation. While the theme of reconciliation had been explored intermittently in the decades before, much of the advances in our understanding of reconciliation can be traced back to what happened in Berlin and throughout Eastern and Central Europe in those days. The undoing of forty years of repression—in many instances, a repression that was built upon a prior history of fascism—seemed a daunting task then, and continues to be so today.

The year 2009 had also been designated by the United Nations as the International Year of Reconciliation. This proclamation was prompted by the awareness that protracted armed conflict has devastated and continues to devastate so much of the world. A renewed effort to overcome the trauma of war and to build a different kind of society—both locally and globally— seemed a particularly apt undertaking at the end of the first decade of the twenty-first century.

Focused more closely on a single continent, a third event brought the theme of reconciliation into the foreground. In October of that year, the Second Special Synod for Africa was celebrated in Rome. Its theme was "The Church in Service to Reconciliation, Justice and Peace." The *lineamenta* and *instrumentum laboris* both recognized how poverty, exploitation, and war have colluded to make contemporary Africa anything but a site of justice and a haven of peace. What is especially significant, from a church perspective, is that the *instrumentum laboris* took the theme of reconciliation beyond its more traditional theological boundaries of sin and penitence.

All in all, a good time to be sojourners on the "roads to reconciliation," as this symposium is intended to be. "The Roads," as a metaphor, suggests that we are indeed on the move, and that there is a certain directionality to our movement. I would like to take up this road metaphor and use it to pose two questions.

The first is: Just where have we come on the road to reconciliation? Taking the International Year of Reconciliation as an opportunity and invitation, I would like to take stock of where we have come and what we have learned over these past twenty years about reconciliation. The learning curve has been a steep one, in many ways—both in the sheer number of events that have called out for reconciliation, and in the density of questions that have emerged from those events. Much of this presentation, therefore, will be given over to charting that road to reconciliation as it has unfolded before us over the past twenty years.

The second question presses one distinctive element in the road metaphor: Are "roads to reconciliation" principally about looking backward—healing the past—or looking forward—building the future? Responding to this question will require a different perspective than the one needed to answer the previous one. It will involve stepping aside, as it were, and trying to locate the multiple discourses of reconciliation within the larger landscape of the past two decades. Why did interest in reconciliation emerge as such a compelling topic when it did? What does it say about what preceded it and what we hope will follow? The final part of this presentation will be devoted to suggesting some responses to that question.

As can be seen from the breadth of these two questions, all I will be able to do here is point to signposts along the road, and not give a thorough treatment of any specific topic. While there is a measure of frustration built into such an approach, this attempt to grasp the big picture has the advantage of offering a wider perspective that might help us address some of the thorny issues involved in reconciliation and perhaps throw some light on puzzlements we experience along the way.

Where Have We Come on the Road to Reconciliation?

"Map is not territory," religion scholar Jonathan Z. Smith reminded us some years ago.[1] A map is an attempt to understand better a terrain and the relationships between its various parts. A roadmap is not the road itself, but a stylized representation that is intended to help us navigate a road's twists and turns, its smooth and its rough parts.

Before embarking on tracing the road to reconciliation, however, it behooves us to consider a bit the territory itself, the terrain that has created the need to chart roads to reconciliation. I have already noted that there was a dramatic increase in events that drew attention to the theme of reconciliation. Just what were those events, and how did they engage the theme of reconciliation in those years? Let me trace briefly some of those events, and note how they provide the contour and texture of the landscape of reconciliation.

I have already mentioned what might be considered the inaugurating event of that period, namely, the end of communism in the countries in East and Central Europe, symbolized in the fall of the Berlin Wall in 1989. The relatively rapid collapse of a whole political and economic order had two seismic effects. First of all, it opened the possibility for the reconstruction of nation-states and their societies now freed from an imposed Marxist–Leninist ideology. The *homo sovieticus*, the "New Man" of the workers' paradise, had turned out to be a hollow figure, lacking the capacity to build a cohesive, vibrant society. The surveillance and terror tactics of state security police had undermined the basic trust needed to have a thriving civil society. The lies that had been proffered as the truth needed to be named and counteracted. Those who had been declared enemies of the state needed to be rehabilitated. All in all, there was a daunting menu of issues that needed addressing before those nation-states could gain some measure of normalcy.

Second, the shifting away from the bipolar geopolitical order allowed a whole series of local conflicts to erupt. Some of these were long-simmering ones, bearing the marks still of the European colonial era. Others were efforts of groups to gain autonomy as nation-states. In the Balkans, in parts of the former Soviet Union, as well in Africa and Asia, conflicts surged throughout the 1990s. What was striking about nearly all of them was that they were armed conflicts within states, rather than between them. The human cost, especially to noncombatants, was often devastatingly high. Peacemaking that entails reinforcing borders was already a familiar solution; but what did peacemaking mean when there were no physical borders, and erstwhile enemies lived next door to one another? The genocide in Rwanda in 1994 became emblematic of the human consequences of such conflicts.

There were other events that contributed to the interest in reconciliation. Nineteen ninety-two was the United Nations' International Year of Indigenous Peoples, marking the five-hundredth anniversary of the arrival of Europeans in the Americas. This prompted native peoples of this hemisphere, as well as peoples in Australia, New Zealand, and some of the Pacific Islands, to set before the world the dehumanizing effects of half a millennium of colonialism and cultural destruction. How to acknowledge and then address these issues, how to think of possible reparations, and how to restore dignity and honor to devastated cultures took on awareness and urgency not previously known.

Nineteen ninety-four was the United Nation's International Year of Women, marked by a World Conference in Beijing. What this event prompted was a new focus on the plight of women and of children around the world. Violence—especially domestic violence—against women and children, human trafficking, and discrimination against women could no longer be treated as a taboo subject. Domestic violence—physical and sexual—was present in every society and every class.

Yet another prominent theme of reconciliation in those years arose out of the end of other kinds of repressive governments—in this case not communist ones, but avowedly anti-communist security states. The end of these governments in Latin America had gained momentum in the 1980s, but the response to their violent pasts was usually one of amnesty and impunity for the wrongdoers. Truth commissions, as an alternative to a war crimes tribunal, had been proposed and were sometimes enacted in many countries, reaching as far back as Bangladesh in the 1970s. But it was the Truth and Reconciliation Commissions (TRC) that convened in Chile, and, thereafter, most dramatically in South Africa, that caught the world's imagination. Imperfect as TRCs have been, they seemed to address, in some measure, the need to set the historic record straight about what had happened, to allow those who had been silenced to speak, and to propose to the successor governments some measures of redress. Today, hardly any conflict ends without a call for such a TRC, although the conditions under which they can be effective are relatively narrow. They have come to be, in the minds of many, one of the few remedies we have at hand to heal wounded pasts.

Two final occurrences that have contributed to the atmosphere of a search for reconciliation deserve mention: one general, one more localized and specific. The general one can be found in the multiple effects of globalization. Alongside its many benefits are a host of negative consequences. The human cost of migration and the plight of immigrants are most noticeable—not that there were not migrants before, but globalization has changed the conditions under which they live. The economic downturn that began in 2008 had some of its most severe effects on those who did the least to cause it. The way wealth is generated and distributed in the global market causes division and polarization. And in the media, the very contrastive nature of how information is transmitted plays into the hands of demagogues and divisive figures. The fact, too, that news transmission is now constant means the conflicts found anywhere are reported everywhere. In the midst of the flood of information, images, and relentless demands for attention, we are discovering that much of our communications media are having a markedly paradoxical effect on the social fabric. Rather than connecting us to one another, we find it dividing us—people are retreating into enclaves of the like-minded and are actually being insulated from pluralism rather than being engaged by it. The polarizing rhetoric that marked so much of the first decade of this new century is a result. Part of the appeal of the Obama presidential campaign for many was the possibility of overcoming this pounding polarization. But as has been seen in the national debate on health care reform, the discourse has remained strident and shrill.

The other area that has impelled some to seek reconciliation is the state of the Roman Catholic Church in the United States. The sexual abuse scandals that began to be reported in 2001 are emblematic of this. Interestingly, a similar wave of sexual abuse had been reported ten years earlier but had not had the same social impact. The anger, alienation, and erosion of trust that the more recent reports evoked come now upon the accumulated anger and alienation caused by a host of other issues besetting the Church (to be sure, some of these are shared with other Christian Churches) regarding authority, teaching, sexuality, and identity.

I have given this extensive list of deep wounds, long-standing grievances, senses of violation, and ruptures of trust to give some idea of the terrain that roads to reconciliation attempt to negotiate. Rebuilding shattered lives, communities, and nations; assuring safety in the most intimate of settings; redressing long-standing crimes against culture and race—all of these have converged, as it were, to create an atmosphere that makes us look to reconciliation as a way through so much pain, suffering, dislocation, and lost opportunities. What the last two decades have done—both for long-standing grievances and misdeeds committed more recently—are create an expectation that something can be done to aright all the wrongs that have been perpetrated against individuals, communities, and nations.

As I look over the terrain that we are being called to traverse, I can discern three roadmaps to reconciliation that have been traced across this territory in the past twenty years. In each of these roadmaps, we learn something about reconciliation itself. We see how the resources—especially of Christian faith—help us negotiate what is often rugged and unforgiving terrain. But we also will see where these roadmaps fall short—where they miscalculate the steep grade that needs to be climbed to attain reconciliation, where they encounter chasms of alienation and suffering that they cannot bridge. Let me turn to them now.

First Roadmap:
Reconciliation Is about the Human Heart

The first roadmap sees reconciliation achieved principally by a conversion of the human heart. Only when we have changed the individuals in a society will there be any hope of changing society itself. Put another way, it is reconciled individuals who will make a reconciled society.

On this view, reconciliation is not something we do, but rather something that God is doing to us. This is certainly the central point of St. Paul's message of reconciliation, our principal source for thinking about a Christian understanding of reconciliation. As he sets forth eloquently in the fifth chapter of the Letter to the Romans, we are reconciled to God because while we were still sinners, Christ died for us (5:8). Paul reminds us here, and elsewhere, that all reconciliation comes from God (2 Cor 5:17), and this reconciliation not only frees us from alienation from God, one another, and the entire cosmos; it also makes of us a "new creation," something utterly transformed.

Such a "vertical" understanding of reconciliation, that is, the relationship between God and all that God has created, has been and continues to be at the very heart of the Church's teaching on reconciliation. It focuses upon how individual wrongdoers are reconciled to their Creator. Liturgical texts and practices of reconciliation all give expression to this teaching.

While such an approach to reconciliation is, for Christians, incontrovertible, it is often difficult to find ways of translating it into "horizontal" reconciliation—reconciliation among human beings, at both the individual and collective level. Here, there is a focus on beginning with the victim and the healing of victims rather than dealing with the perpetrator. While Christians believe that it is only God who has the perspicacity to comprehend the enormity of evil and the consequences of evildoing, the emphasis on the repentance of the wrongdoer runs into the fact that, in human realities, wrongdoers often do not and will not repent. Where does that leave the victims?

A more victim-centered approach to reconciliation is, of course, possible within the framework of Christian faith. The option for the poor and the accompaniment of those who are marginalized, as exemplified in the message of the Hebrew prophets and in the praxis of Jesus, provide an ample base. Much recent effort in developing a theology of reconciliation has been trying to explore these possibilities. Yet to date, there has been little liturgical support for the care of victims. The apologies Pope John Paul II offered within the context of Evening Prayer on the first Sunday of Lent in 2000 are at least a harbinger of what might still come.

The *instrumentum laboris* for the Synod for Africa gave a very good summary of this first road to reconciliation, based on the conversion of human hearts. Although it encourages acts of advocacy, charity, and education, it centers on the sacraments and the growth in holiness of individuals as the key to reconciliation in Africa. There is a deep truth here: without a cadre of truly reconciled individuals, one cannot hope to transform a society. As an example, one can speculate what the end of the apartheid era in South Africa might have looked like were it not for the vision of Nelson Mandela and the way Desmond Tutu led the Truth and Reconciliation Commission. But at the same time, focusing only on the state of grace of individuals does not seem to begin to reach far enough into the huge problems that Africa faces today—problems that are also outlined at the beginning of the *instrumentum laboris*: crushing poverty, cycles of famine, protracted warfare, and endemic corruption in societies.

To focus on individual conversion and union with God is an essential part of any road to reconciliation (from a Christian perspective), but it by itself fails to account for other important features. A society is more than the sum of individuals, and what is called social or structural sin cannot be reduced to the accumulated sins of individuals. To speak of reconciliation only in terms of individual conversion does not adequately deal with the kind of society that needs to emerge from conversion. The flawed character of a view of reconciliation focused only on individuals has been evident for a long time in the ecclesial and educational ministries of the Church: regular reception of the sacraments and a Catholic education do not inoculate a society against evil practices. The majority of the *genocidaires* in Rwanda, after all, were Christian—most of them Catholic.

To make the same point in more individual terms: advising a battered spouse to solve the problem of being beaten by praying more and forgiving her spouse does not solve the problem of domestic violence. Some demons may be driven out by prayer and fasting (Matt 17:21), but others are not. Put another way, the tangled roots of violence and wrongdoing cannot be reduced to individual sin, even though sin is undeniably a part of the equa-

21

tion. Moreover, pastorally, the sole focus on the human heart is likely to sound like advice to endure one's suffering rather than work in some way to overcome it.

So as a roadmap to reconciliation, to see reconciliation only as something about the individual human heart will not in itself get us to our goal. To put it in philosophical language, the conversion of the individual heart is a necessary but not sufficient condition for reconciliation. It provides an important, indeed indispensable resource, and is an important feature for orientation on the road to reconciliation. But we need more.

Roadmap Two:
Reconciliation Is about Overcoming Injustice

A second roadmap to achieve reconciliation takes a different approach, building somewhat on the perceived shortcomings of the first roadmap. This second approach addresses the complexity of causes that create situations that call for reconciliation. It focuses especially on social factors, and their accumulated, historical effects upon a situation. It tries to discern how different forms of wrongdoing become intertwined and become, over time, nearly impossible to untangle. In nations, histories of colonialism or foreign subjugation are kept in place by endemic poverty and protracted conflict. The dysfunctional systems of families can affect family members for generation after generation. Institutions, intended to be beneficent, develop repressive and oppressive features that become embedded in their culture. In a word, there are glaring absences of right relations we call together injustice.

The road to reconciliation can be construed as a struggle against injustice. A cry that is often heard in the aftermath of repression in a country is that there can be no reconciliation without an end to injustice, and indeed a punishment of wrongdoers. Pope Paul VI's oft-quoted dictum "If you want peace, work for justice" sums this up succinctly. Especially since the 1970 Synod of Bishops on Justice in the World, and parallel efforts in the World Council of Churches beginning about the same time, the work for reconciliation has often focused on the work for justice. Pope John Paul II reiterated this teaching in his 2002 Message for the World Day of Peace when he said that the two pillars that support peace are justice and forgiveness.

As well it should. The language of "reconciliation" often can be found on the lips of wrongdoers who want victims to forget the past and the sufferings victims have endured. It is a way of skipping over the issue of justice. The use of amnesty and impunity in Latin America in the 1980s made "reconciliation" a bad word in many of those countries. Justice is clearly understood as one of the central attributes of God in all three of the Abrahamic faiths. The Bible (and the Qur'an) is filled with references to justice.

Without some measure of justice, the wounds of those who have suffered injustice cannot heal. Without the continuing pursuit of justice, efforts and programs of reconciliation will not have authenticity in the eyes of victims. But even more important here than the authenticity that makes for credibility is a faithfulness to God and to God's work in reconciliation. And that work is inconceivable without a continuing pursuit of justice.

At the same time, twenty years in the work of reconciliation has taught us a few things about the pursuit of justice—especially our pursuit of justice as it might be compared to God's own justice. There are three things in particular that we have learned that need to be mentioned here. The first is when justice focuses exclusively on punitive justice, that is, the punishment of wrongdoers; it is inadequate at best and can become deleterious to the entire process of reconciliation and healing at worst. The punishment of wrongdoers can serve a deeply felt human impulse (Jared Diamond and evolutionary psychologists have ranked it among the basic "adaptive responses" that have shaped human social behavior since we lived in small bands of hunter-gatherers) for retaliation when we have been harmed. Retaliation is intended to deter the wrongdoer from striking again, and fits into a larger social pattern that sees society as an equilibrium among competing, hostile forces. In Western societies, this primitive adaptive response is often depicted as Dame Justice holding a set of scales, blindfolded to indicate her impartiality in restoring balance in society. Sociologists studying Western societies have cast considerable doubt on whether punishment for the sake of deterrence actually does create the hoped-for block on future wrongful behavior. Yet, it remains an important mechanism at the very least for maintaining the state's claim to monopoly on violence in society.

From the point of view of reconciliation, punitive justice runs the risk of not actually stopping cycles of violence, but merely sending them into gestation until the opportunity arises for the punished to retaliate against those doing the punishing. Perhaps one of the most graphic examples of this at a social level in the twentieth century was the punishment meted out against Germany by the Allies at the end of the First World War. The heavy fines, the wresting away of territory, and the military occupation of the Rhineland was intended to punish and to humiliate. Many historians consider this experience as preparing the ground for accepting fascism in that country, so much so that recent histories of the period suggest that the twenty years between 1919 and 1939 was but a truce in one, continuous war.

Enacting punitive justice has the decided positive effect of saying that the state will not tolerate such wrongdoing in the future. But it largely fails to create the conditions for a different kind of society; it can only produce its mirror opposite, of not tolerating such acts. It is in light of this that movements for restorative justice have taken on more significance in peace studies, not only in criminal justice systems but also in thinking about the reconstruction of society as a whole.

Worse, a single-minded pursuit of punitive justice can actually make long-term conditions for full reconciliation worse. A much-debated point in this regard at the moment is the warrant issued by the International Criminal Court for the arrest of the President of the Sudan, Omar al-Bashir. He has retaliated by expelling aid agencies that are keeping more than a million people in Darfur alive. One of the dangers in the pursuit of justice in complex situations of wrongdoing is that the concept of justice can become exceedingly abstract, and so do damage to concrete realities rather than ameliorating the conditions and direct experiences of injustice.

A second and related feature of the limits of justice has to do with being able to deal with the cascading effects of long-term injustice. Wrongdoing, social sin, and all their consequences become so interlaced and entrenched in societies that they become almost impossible to eradicate. We chip away at them as it were, either through focusing on individual injustices, or by enacting structural changes that we hope will erase the conditions under which injustice continues to operate. Think, for example, of the ongoing struggle against racism in this country. Four decades of addressing individual projects, especially in education, and of enacting legislation to counteract discrimination have brought us as a nation a long way. Barack Obama would never have been elected president without it. Yet we are constantly reminded of how much has to be done, and the vigilance needed to keep from sliding back to an earlier state. Such a realization should not make us give up on the pursuit of justice—on the contrary. But it makes us realize how focused we need to continue to be. We cannot achieve perfect justice. And what does that mean for the healing process within reconciliation?

A third consideration about the limits of justice grows out of another thing we are learning about reconciliation. Reconciliation is about change. We have long known that it involves the change of the wrongdoer and calls for a series of actions on the wrongdoer's part: remorse, apology, asking for forgiveness, a willingness to accept punishment or to engage in acts of expiation. But what has become clearer over time is that the victim, too, has to undergo change if there is to be a "new creation." I am not talking here about blaming victims for the plight in which they find themselves. But at some point, victims have to be willing to engage the harm that has been done them, so as to secure—at the very least—a return of the agency that has been wrested away from them to change their relationship to what has happened: to the deed, the wrongdoer, and the larger setting in which all of this happened. We know that the reconstruction of life after grievous harm and irretrievable loss requires a new set of relationships to oneself, the community, to the past, and even to God. The repair of the web of meaning that situates in a life-giving, interdependent world requires all of this. Often in the pursuit of justice, there is a sense that change is only something for the wrongdoer. If that change happens, the integrity of the victim is restored. That is, of course, too simple. It rests on the belief that grave injustice and wrongdoing can simply be erased or removed from the lives of victims without any further consequences for those victims, and the victims can then return to a *status quo ante* and continue life as though nothing ever happened. But profound misdeeds change our lives inalterably. We cannot bring back the dead. We cannot restore a way of life and some networks of relationships that have been irretrievably taken from us. To pursue justice without regard for the change that will have to happen in the lives of victims, will only eventuate in a one-sided, inadequate enactment of justice.

I raise these points about the limits of justice to show the limits of this kind of roadmap for achieving reconciliation. In circles where reconciliation is being pursued, inadequate and abstract pursuits of justice can actually hamper the longer-term quest for reconciliation and healing. An example would be the 1997 meeting of the European Council of Churches in Graz. The meeting, intended to explore reconciliation, broke down into competing lobbying groups for different causes, each claiming that the injustices that they had suffered were the most grievous and, therefore, had to have priority of attention. The World Council of Churches, in some of its documents in that period, had made the pursuit of justice such a central priority that it became impossible to make any other move toward a wider reconciliation short of complete justice. Miroslav Volf, one of the most sensitive students of reconciliation, pointed this out at the time.[2]

Like seeing the conversion of the individual human heart as

the best roadmap to reconciliation, the pursuit of justice as yet another roadmap carries with it deep truths that we ignore at our own peril. But as the sole roadmap, it may not help us negotiate some of the terrain on the road to reconciliation. When one deals with long-term wrongdoing and the accumulation of the effects of social sin, the pursuit of justice becomes a necessary, but not in itself sufficient, condition for reaching reconciliation. If left only to changing the wrongdoing that has been done and eliminating the conditions that sustain injustice, it may not deal adequately with the other changes that must mark wrongdoers and victims alike.

Roadmap Three:
Reconciliation Is about Alternative Social Formations

A third roadmap to reconciliation grows out of two sets of experiences. The first set arises from the realization of the strengths and weaknesses of the two roadmaps already discussed. Both roadmaps have provided indispensable guideposts on the road to reconciliation, focusing upon the conversion of individual hearts and the pursuit of justice. As we have come to experience the complexity of reconciliation processes—be it in international peacemaking or dealing with polarizations within Church and society—we have also become aware of the limitations of the roadmaps these provide for all the varieties of terrain that a road to reconciliation must negotiate. Hence, the limitations have caused us to ask questions.

The second set of experiences has to do with what has been found to "work" in reconciliation efforts over the past twenty years. Truth and Reconciliation Commissions, for example, have existed at least since 1970. But it was the TRCs in Chile and South Africa that have captured the wider imagination. Efforts at healing of memories, such as the REMHI Project in Guatemala, have also been turned to increasingly as an important avenue to national healing. The growing attention given to processes of forgiveness constitutes yet another venue for reconciliation.

This leads me to propose consideration of a third kind of roadmap to achieving reconciliation. I call it "alternative social formations." Alternative social formations are sites of liminal performance, often highly ritualized in nature, that provide spaces for engaging in practices that promote reconciliation. They are spaces that are alternative, in that they are not located entirely in the present (therefore, only accompanying the victim or wrongdoer in their present state), in the past (therefore, dealing with memory and the healing of memory), nor only in the future (imagining or engaging in utopian thinking). Rather they are spaces that allow for movement between all three of these dimensions of time. That movement is made possible by recourse to ritual, a performance that can link these different dimensions in such a way as to make each and all of them "present" to us.

These spaces have been identified by thinkers such as postcolonial theorist Homi Bhabha as "third spaces" wherein reigning patterns of power and domination are deconstructed and even reversed.[3] Anthropologist Paul Rabinow speaks of "interstitial" zones, where people come out of their own bounded situations to meet one another in a place that bears some of the marks of their home territory, but is really a new place.[4]

These spaces are primarily *social* spaces, rather than physical ones—although specific physical sites may become the locales for these social spaces (think of monuments to the dead or public sites where profound social changes began to take place, such as the remains of the Berlin Wall). These spaces are constituted principally by the people who gather there with the intent of enacting something relating to the process of reconciliation. They are "provisional," both in the sense of temporary, and also in the sense of providing something that the current social environment lacks or cannot bring forward. As such, they are primarily social, rather than physical formations.

Take, for example, the Thursday demonstrations in the Plaza de Mayo in Buenos Aires by the mothers of the disappeared. These demonstrations eventually brought down the *junta* in

Argentina in 1983, and continued for more than twenty years to call attention to the continuing need to pursue justice. After impunity of the wrongdoers from the dirty war was lifted, these demonstrations linked the nation back twenty years to the times of the wrongdoing itself. It might be helpful to mention here other examples. I have already noted Truth and Reconciliation Commissions, and the REMHI Project in Guatemala at the end of the civil war there. Here are some others:

- The use of "healing" or "listening" circles to help individuals deal with their wounds as victims. There, victims gather in safe and hospitable spaces to examine their traumatic pasts and seek new narratives to tell their stories.
- Creating a new social space in the midst of conflict, such as that of Appreciative Inquiry, that begins by looking at the positive achievements rather than the failures of a community.[5]
- Creating alternative venues and modes of healing through athletics and music, especially for youth.[6]
- Building monuments to the dead, such as the *Ojo que Llora* in Lima, or the Vietnam Veterans Memorial in Washington, DC, or at Ground Zero in New York City, provide a space where survivors can come to mourn their dead.
- Efforts of the Catholic Common Ground Initiative, a program for reconciliation that Cardinal Bernardin established at the very end of his life, is one of the enduring examples of alternative social formations.

I do not want to give the impression that all alternative social formations are highly formalized undertakings, such as some of those that I have mentioned. Sometimes they are moments within other activities. I am thinking here of Archbishop Desmond Tutu's exhortations to forgiveness given regularly during sessions of the South African Truth and Reconciliation Commission, or rituals many women's groups have developed to heal from abuse, increase individual agency, or form life-giving communities.

The point of focusing upon these alternative social formations is to call attention to some important insights about reconciliation and the road to reconciliation that the last two decades have given us. Attending to these alternative social formations help highlight some of these realizations. Let me try to enumerate some of them for you here:

1. We sometimes focus inordinately on reconciliation as a goal and forget how much of it is a process. That process is not simply a means to an end; that is, something we do and then discard upon reaching the goal. It is also part of the goal itself. If reconciliation is about change in all the parties involved, that change is more than a matter of mind. It is inscribed in our bodies. Alternative social formations are the inscribing moments.

2. Even though we are speaking of the "road" to reconciliation, reconciliation as a goal is rarely reached by a linear process. There are many reversals, doublings back, twists and turns, dead ends, and other detours along the way. The repetitive character of these alternative social formations remind us of this and embed the practices of reconciliation within the social fabric, not as a once-for-all event, but a recurrent (although we also hope, cumulative) process toward an end.

3. This non-linear quality of reconciliation holds, not only for our spatial experience, but also for our experience of time as well. We find ourselves turning back to the past as our present changes, re-imagining an already imagined future. The ritual quality of many alternative social formations helps us negotiate this moving in and out of different experiences of time.

4. Reconciliation as a goal can only be partially imagined. We cannot envision it entirely ahead of time or project the present experience into the future. As

such, our experience of reconciliation is always incomplete. From a Christian point of view, we yearn for eschatological fulfillment, when "God may be all in all" (1 Cor 15:28).

I hope these general suggestions give some idea of what I am coming to believe is an important part of the work of reconciliation, namely, attending to the role of alternative social formations as a constituent part of the process. It gives us a different roadmap through the terrain of healing and reconciliation, having as a particular strength an appreciation of the role of the practices of reconciliation as moments of an anticipatory experience of reconciliation, as well as signposts of just how far we have come and still need to go.

At the same time, such an approach, too, has its limitations. One can come to dwell in these alternative social formations as a kind of haven on a painful path, and not want to leave their provisional comforts. One can become transfixed by the moments of healing in such a way as not to be willing to continue the onward journey. As a roadmap, these alternative social formations do change our perception of the contours of the terrain. But again, map is not territory.

Conclusion: Healing the Past or Building the Future?

I return to a question raised at the beginning: Is reconciliation about healing the past or building the future? In a road that is as much marked by paradox as another trope, the answer is: yes. Both are essential dimensions. To be sure, depending upon the terrain that needs to be traversed, there may be more emphasis on one than the other. For the generation that has experienced acute loss and trauma, the past may be preeminent. For their children and grandchildren, the future may be the preoccupation. The nature of wounds that wrongdoing wreaks upon the human heart

31

and the human community remind us that no single dimension will suffice for the healing. Healing is something that must embrace all of the dimensions of the human condition and the human journey. I hope that your experience in this symposium will help you achieve both: healing of the past—as many of the workshops will be addressing—and hope for the future, upon which other of the workshops will be focusing. May your journeys today on the road to reconciliation bring you, in the words of the title of the Synod for Africa, both salt and light.

Notes

1. Jonathan Z. Smith, *Map Is Not Territory: Studies in the History of Religions* (Leiden: Brill, 1978).

2. Miroslav Volf, "The Social Meaning of Reconciliation," *Interpretation* 54 (2000): 158–72.

3. Homi Bhabha, *The Location of Culture* (London: Routledge, 1994), 37.

4. Paul Rabinow, *Reflections on Fieldwork in Morocco* (Berkeley: University of California Press, 1977).

5. See, in this regard, William Nordenbrock, *Beyond Accompaniment: Guiding a Fractured Community to Wholeness* (Collegeville, MN: Liturgical Press, 2011), which discusses how a parish that was riven with division over parish mergers and then revelations of sexual abuse by the pastor found its way to reconciliation.

6. See the accounts in David Little, ed., *Peacemakers in Action: Profiles of Religion in Conflict Resolution* (Cambridge: Cambridge University Press, 2007).

3

WHAT DOES THE NEW TESTAMENT SAY ABOUT RECONCILIATION?

Thomas Stegman, SJ

A quick glance at a New Testament concordance indicates that Paul is a primary source for investigating what the New Testament has to say about reconciliation. Thirteen of the sixteen instances of reconciliation terminology in the NRSV appear in the Pauline writings.[1] As we will see, reconciliation is an important theme for Paul in his proclamation of the Gospel as well as in his understanding of the new covenant ministry. All the same, an examination of what the New Testament has to say about reconciliation must go beyond explicit references. Indeed, Jesus' parables contribute much, at least implicitly, to the New Testament's teaching about reconciliation.

This essay consists of three parts. Part One treats God's role in reconciling the world to himself. It, thus, deals with the vertical dimension of reconciliation, the restored relationship that exists (at least potentially) between God and human beings, and focuses on what reconciliation reveals about the character and nature of God. Part Two then turns to the horizontal dimension of reconciliation, that is, to how God's act of reconciliation has created new and life-giving ways for people to be in communion with one another. Finally, Part Three offers a brief analysis of how Paul enacts the message and ministry of reconciliation in his dealings with the newly founded church in Corinth.

Part One:
God and the Vertical Dimension
of Reconciliation

In order to fully appreciate what is meant by reconciliation terminology, it is necessary to look at the context this language presumes. Reconciliation presumes a prior context of *enmity*— enmity between nations, between citizens, or even between estranged friends and spouses. The act of reconciliation ultimately entails a change in social relationship. At the human level, this change in relationship is aptly expressed by the exchange of friendship. A distinguishing feature of the act of reconciliation between former enemies is the resulting condition of peace.

Paul draws on and adapts this conceptual background. In 2 Corinthians 5:18–19, he states that God has "reconciled us to himself through Christ...; that is, in Christ God was reconciling the world to himself, not counting their trespasses against them..."[2] Paul's proclamation contains several noteworthy features. One is that he reveals here what was the source of enmity between God and human beings: namely, sin. This is evident from Paul's explanatory statement that God's act of reconciliation means 'not counting trespasses against' those who receive the gospel in faith. What Paul presumes is that sin—understood most fundamentally as "ungodliness," that is, as people's refusal to glorify God and to obey his designs for them (cf. Rom 1:18–23)—has ruptured the relationship between God and humanity. But unlike typical situations of enmity between peoples, in which both sides bear (at least some of the) blame for the breakdown in relationship, here it was only one party—humanity—that caused the rupture. Nevertheless, Paul teaches that God, who was the "offended" party, is the one who took the initiative to make right what had gone wrong when human beings rebelled. Indeed, only God could heal and restore the divine–human relationship. God's initiative in reconciling humanity to himself reveals his gracious forbearance and magnanimity.

Another noteworthy feature of Paul's teaching is the central role played by Jesus in God's act of reconciliation. Most of the Pauline references to reconciliation allude to Jesus' death on the cross, such as Colossians 1:20: "God was pleased to reconcile to himself all things...through the blood of [Jesus'] cross" (cf. Rom 5:9–10; Eph 2:16).[3] While this sacrificial imagery makes some people uneasy, it is important to recognize how Paul understands the role of divine *love* at work here. In the first place, that God enacts the work of reconciliation through his Son reveals that God himself holds nothing back in manifesting his love for us: "If God is for us, who is against us? He who did not withhold his own Son, but gave him up for all of us, will he not with him also give us everything else?" (Rom 8:31b–32). For Paul, Jesus is the revelation of God's love (Rom 5:8; cf John 3:16). In the second place, Jesus makes known God's love by his own manner of self-giving existence, one that culminates in his holding nothing back—not even his very life—in showing forth his love (Eph 5:2). There is a dynamic synergy between God's love and Jesus' love, a synergy of love that grounds God's act of reconciliation through Christ. Such love has brought about a "new creation" (2 Cor 5:17), and now results in the gift of peace (Col 1:20).

One of Paul's great contributions to "soteriology," the study of salvation, is the central role he gives to reconciliation. Paul employs many images and terms to express the richness of the mystery of salvation—of what God has done for humankind through the life, death, and resurrection of Jesus—such as justification, redemption, and transformation. Justification (by faith) has often been privileged as expressing Paul's major emphasis. That is a debated point today among theologians and exegetes. For our purposes here, it is sufficient to note how Paul employs the notions of justification and reconciliation in parallel fashion in Romans 5:9–10: "Much more surely then, now that we have been justified by his blood, will we be saved through him from the wrath of God. For if while we were enemies, we were reconciled to God through the death of his Son, much more surely, having been reconciled, will we be saved by his life." The significant point is that reconciliation is an essential aspect of Paul's proclamation of the gospel. And as we will see below, it is also one of the major tasks given to the Church.

Paul's is not the only word on reconciliation in the New Testament, however. To be sure, reconciliation terminology appears in the Gospels only in Matthew 5:24. All the same, Jesus teaches much about the reconciling character of God in two of his more memorable parables. In Matthew 18:23–35, in the parable of the unforgiving servant, Jesus presents an image of "grace beyond imagining."[4] He tells of a king who wished to settle accounts with his servants. One servant had so mismanaged affairs that he owed the king "ten thousand talents." The word *myria*, "ten thousand," signifies the largest conceivable number, so what Jesus indicates here is that the servant in question owed an exorbitant debt. Although it was impossible for him to pay it back in full, he still fell on his knees and asked the king for patience, promising to make recompense. It is the king's response that merits our attention: he is moved with "pity" or, better, compassion, and forgives his servant the debt, wiping it completely off the books. Jesus, thereby, reveals God's merciful nature that tempers and qualifies his justice.

The second parable through which Jesus illustrates God's compassionate character is found in Luke 15:11–32, the famous parable of the prodigal son, sometimes called the parable of the prodigal father because of the latter's lavish response to his penitent son. The story is so familiar to us that it is easy to pass over details over which we are invited to linger. One detail not to be overlooked is the notice that the father saw his son "while he was still far off." The point is not that the father just happened one day, by coincidence, to catch a glimpse of his wayward son. Rather, the image suggests that the father was constantly at vigil, looking out at the horizon, hoping and waiting for his son to return home. And when he sees the humbled and bedraggled young man, the father's heart is "filled with compassion" (the verb is the same as in the previous parable). The father casts aside all social conventions and runs to embrace his son (it would have been considered beneath the dignity of a prominent man to do so). He covers the young man with kisses and, through the bestowal of new clothing and a ring, restores him to the status he had forfeited when he ungratefully demanded his share of the inheritance and left home. Rembrandt's famous depiction of this scene captures well the loving mercy of God that Jesus wants to express by this parable, the mercy through which God restores the divine relationship that was ruptured by sin.

Part Two:
The Horizontal Dimension
of Reconciliation

While God's intervention through Christ's death (and resurrection) has brought about the healing and restoration of the relationship between God and human beings—one that must be appropriated in faith by each individual—there is more involved in the work of reconciliation. In addition to this vertical dimension, reconciliation also entails a horizontal dimension, the healing and restoration of relationships between peoples.

According to Paul, the human rebellion against God's designs for humanity also resulted in the breakdown of human relationships, a breakdown marked by egocentrism, injustice, malice, and violence (see esp. Rom 1:29–31). One manifestation of the divided state of humanity was, from a Jewish perspective, the division of peoples into Jews and Gentiles, a division that was often marked by enmity. Paul, who was born and raised a Jew and who maintained his Jewish identity after his call from the risen Christ (Rom 9:3; 2 Cor 11:22), came to appreciate that God's action through Jesus has brought about a new possibility for human relationships: Christ "is our peace; in his flesh he has made both groups [i.e., Jews and Gentiles] into one and has broken down the dividing wall, that is, the hostility between us" (Eph 2:14). Christ offered himself in love so that "he might create in himself one new humanity in place of the two, thus making peace, and might reconcile both groups to God in one body..." (Eph 2:15–16). The "dividing wall" in Eph 2:14 is an allusion to the barrier at the Jerusalem temple that separated the court of the Gentiles from the inner courts, a barrier beyond which Gentiles could not pass.[5] It became, for Paul, a symbol of divided humanity, a division that Christ has broken down.

One of Paul's most famous statements in regard to reconciliation concerns his assessment of those who have been baptized and who have, thus, clothed themselves with Christ: "There is no longer Jew or Greek, there is no longer slave or free, there is no longer male and female; for all of you are one in Christ Jesus" (Gal 3:28). Paul signifies here at least four ways in which human beings are stratified: ethnic differences ("Jew or Greek"); religious differences ("Jew or Greek"); socioeconomic differences ("slave or free"); and gender differences ("male and female"). His point is not that these differences have been obliterated by Christ. Rather, what Paul insists on is that these differences no longer need or should be occasions for driving wedges between peoples; they no longer need or should be occasions for oppressing anyone. Christ has brought about a new possibility for human relationships, that of being fellow children of God and, therefore, brothers and sisters. Paul was passionate that members of the churches he founded truly regard one another as brothers and sisters in Christ. For him, the great miracle of what God has done through Christ is to bring about the possibility of unity-in-diversity that characterizes the Christian community as "the body of Christ" (cf. 1 Cor 12:4–31). A quick glance at Paul's exhortations to the churches he founded shows that he was mostly concerned with attitudes and behaviors that build up the community (e.g., Rom 14:19; 1 Cor 14:12; 1 Thess 5:11). The most compelling witness to the efficacy of the gospel is a community that reflects how Christ has empowered the possibility of vastly diverse peoples living as a single, reconciled "family."

Returning to the parables treated in Part One, we see how Jesus also treats the horizontal dimension of reconciliation. The tragedy of the parable of the unforgiving servant (Matt 18:23–35) is that the man who was forgiven a debt he could never repay later refuses to have mercy on a fellow servant, one who owes a mere pittance and who cries for compassion in the very same words: "Have patience with me, and I will pay you everything" (18:26, 29). The unforgiving servant is then severely punished when the king learns about his lack of compassion. Jesus, thereby, teaches that the reconciliation and forgiveness God bestows on us is to be extended to our fellow human beings. It is significant that Jesus offers this parable—prompted by Peter's question, "[H]ow often should I forgive?" (18:21)—in the midst of his discourse on what life in the Christian community should look like. One distinguishing mark of the Christian community is the willingness of its members to forgive one another. The "logic" of reconciliation is that those who are reconciled to God are to grow in being reconciled with one another. That the willingness to forgive others is in fact the task of Christians is clear from one of the petitions in the prayer Jesus taught his disciples: "[F]orgive us our debts, as we also have forgiven our debtors" (Matt 6:12). In fact, so urgent is this charge that Jesus exhorts his followers, if necessary, to leave behind an offering on the altar and "first be reconciled to your brother or sister" (Matt 5:24). There is no authentic appropriation of the vertical dimension of reconciliation if one does not participate in the horizontal dimension.

There is also tragedy in the Lucan parable of the prodigal son/father (15:11–32). In this case, the older brother's attitude and behavior are negative foils for what Jesus intends to inculcate. The older brother—who it must be said has manifested loyalty to his father—falls prey to self-righteousness (15:29—"For all these years I have been working like a slave for you...") and to judgmentalism (15:30—cf. his statement about the younger brother's squandering the inheritance on prostitutes, a detail that Jesus does not explicitly report). The older brother, thus, reveals—by negative example—that we are called to recognize our own need for mercy and compassion. Doing so will help preclude the temptation to set oneself in the position of judge over another (cf. Luke 6:37–38a—"Do not judge, and you will not be judged; do not condemn, and you will not be condemned. Forgive, and you will be forgiven…"). What is worse, the older brother also, in effect, disowns his younger sibling, as he disdainfully refers to the latter as "this son of yours" (15:30). The father insists, however, that the prodigal son is still in fact "this brother of yours" (15:32). The parable ends without reporting whether the older brother joined in the celebration of the younger brother's return. The effect of this open-endedness is to challenge us to open our hearts to receive back and support as brothers and sisters those who repent of wrongdoing. The unity and well-being of the "family," of the Christian community, depend on such reconciliation.

Part Three:
Exemplification of the
"Ministry of Reconciliation"

God's work of reconciling the world through Christ is more than a theological datum. Paul makes clear that God's work of reconciliation is ongoing and that it is offered through the ministry of the Church. Indeed, in the passage in which Paul sets forth his teaching of God's reconciling initiative, he also reveals that God has entrusted "the ministry of reconciliation" and "the message of reconciliation to us"—that is, to ministers like him and, by extension, to the Church as a whole (2 Cor 5:18–19). For Paul, the ministry of reconciliation is an expression par excellence of the ministry in which those who are called to be "ministers of a new covenant" of the life-giving Spirit (2 Cor 3:6) are to participate.

Paul participates in the ministry of reconciliation, in the first place, by proclaiming the gospel. It is telling that he regards himself and his co-workers—and ministers in general—as "ambassadors for Christ" (2 Cor 5:20). Paul speaks and acts, not on his own accord, but as an envoy of Jesus. And just as Jesus, in his life and ministry, revealed God's word, so now, through Christ, God makes his appeal through Paul (and ministers like him): "Be reconciled to God!" Thus, the ministry of proclaiming the gospel has at its heart the invitation to people to receive the gift of a renewed relationship with God through Christ, the vertical dimension of reconciliation.

But Paul does more than proclaim God's work of reconciliation; he also *enacts* it at the horizontal level. This is most clearly exhibited in his dealings with the church in Corinth.[6] Paul's relationship with (at least some members of) the community had become strained. A number of circumstances conspired to create the situation. While it is impossible to reconstruct with certitude the various factors at play, it seems that one factor involved a painful incident during a visit Paul paid to Corinth. A certain member confronted him and insolently challenged his authority; what made matters worse was that the community did not immediately come to his defense. Stunned, Paul left the city and later wrote a letter, which is no longer extant, in which he expressed his love and concern for the community, as well as his disappointment over what had transpired (2 Cor 2:3-4). Upon hearing Paul's side of things, the Corinthians repented of their complicit silence and took action against the offending member by punishing him (7:10-11), probably by ostracizing him and excluding him from table fellowship.

When Paul learns about this punishment, he exhorts the community to "forgive and console" the offender and to "reaffirm [their] love" for him (2 Cor 2:7-8). The verb translated "reaffirm" is a legal term that denotes an official rescindment of punishment. Noteworthy here is Paul's magnanimity, as he looks past his own hurt to consider the pain and plight of the punished man. Paul goes on to indicate that he has already forgiven the offender (2:10), thereby modeling the reconciliation to which he exhorts the community. He then reminds the Corinthians that it is Satan's design to rend the Christian community asunder by dividing its members (2:11); hence the importance of reconciliation.

Another factor that strained the relationship between Paul and the Corinthians had to do with money. Paul was committed to preach the gospel "free of charge" (2 Cor 11:7), that is, he did not take direct remuneration from those to whom he ministered. This practice dismayed some wealthier members of the community who, in an honor and shame culture, desired the "honor" of sponsoring the work of the apostle. Their dismay increased when it was learned that Paul was receiving financial support from other churches for his ministry in Corinth (11:9). It seemed to some there that Paul was playing favorites. Further complicating things was that he was asking the community to be generous for a collection he was taking up for the church in Jerusalem (8:1–9:15), a church that was in dire economic need. Mistrust arose because, on the one hand, Paul insisted on not taking direct payment from the Corinthians while, on the other hand, he took contributions from other churches and was now soliciting a special collection.

Paul's way of clarifying these financial issues exhibits his commitment to reconciliation. He explains to the Corinthians that his practice of preaching the gospel free of charge is itself an expression of the gratuitous nature of the gospel—of God's initiative in making right what had gone wrong through human sin. Paul was committed to "gladly spend and be spent" for the church in Corinth because of his great love for them (2 Cor 12:15). However, he was happy to receive financial assistance from churches that would aid his ministry elsewhere. In fact, Paul praised the church in Philippi for their generosity to his missionary work, a generosity he regarded as their "sharing in the gospel" (Phil 1:5). What Paul exemplifies in his dealings with the Corinthians is the importance of "clearing the air" when misunderstandings arise. Then, as now, misunderstandings over financial and other temporal concerns can derail the work of ministry. Paul patiently explains and clarifies his ways to the Corinthians, making sure they understand that his "heart is wide open to you" (2 Cor 6:11). Sometimes it is necessary for ministers to recognize that the work of reconciliation must begin with attending to their own relationship with their communities.

Moreover, Paul understood the collection for the church in Jerusalem to be a sign of the reconciliation between peoples that God has brought about through Christ. To be sure, the collection would provide much needed financial help to a suffering community. Even more, it would express *koinōnia*—"communion"— between the predominantly Gentile churches he had founded and the Jewish–Christian foundation in Jerusalem. As Paul explains to the Christians in Rome, because the Gentiles have come to share in the spiritual blessings that have emanated from the church in Jerusalem, so now should they be of service in responding to the material needs of the mother church (Rom 15:27). Paul's painstaking labors to bring the collection to Jerusalem were intended to proclaim how God, through Christ, had broken down the dividing wall between Gentiles and Jews (Eph 2:14): they are now truly brothers and sisters in Christ. The ministry of reconciliation, thus, calls communities to look beyond themselves to attend to the needs of others.

Conclusion

The New Testament teaches that reconciliation begins with God. Through the self-giving love of Jesus, culminating with his death on the cross, God has acted to reach out and reconcile the world to himself. The source of reconciliation is God's compassionate, merciful love, his impetus to make right what has gone wrong through human sin. The restoration of the divine–human relationship also involves the healing of relationships between human beings. Indeed, the authentic appropriation of the vertical dimension of reconciliation requires a commitment to the horizontal dimension, to the healing of the divisions and enmity among peoples. The mark of a person who has truly received

God's mercy and forgiveness is to become more merciful and forgiving in turn. The Christian community is to be the place where reconciliation is both practiced and imaged forth for others to see.

Notes

1. The NRSV translates the following compounds of the verb *allassō* as "reconcile": *diallassō* (Matt 5:24); *synallassō* (Acts 7:26); *katallassō* (Rom 5:10 [2x]; 1 Cor 7:11; 2 Cor 5:18; 5:19; 5:20); and *apokatallassō* (Eph 2:16; Col 1:20; 1:22). It renders both the noun *katallagē* (Rom 5:11; 11:15; 2 Cor 5:18; 5:19) and the phrase *aiteō eirēnēn* (literally, "to ask for peace"; Acts 12:20) as "reconciliation."

2. All scriptural quotations in this article are from the NRSV.

3. The authorship of the Letters to the Colossians and Ephesians is disputed. I regard Paul to be the author of both epistles. Among those who question Pauline authorship, it should be noted that the majority consider these letters to be faithful expressions of the apostle's central concerns.

4. The phrase is taken from M. Eugene Boring, "The Gospel of Matthew: Introduction, Commentary, and Reflections," in *The New Interpreter's Bible*, ed. Leander E. Keck et al., vol. 8 (Nashville: Abingdon, 1995), 380.

5. For more on the dividing wall, see Margaret Y. MacDonald, *Colossians and Ephesians*, Sacra Pagina 17 (Collegeville, MN: The Liturgical Press, 2000), 244–45.

6. For more on Paul's pastoral sensitivity and strategies in connection with "the ministry of reconciliation" throughout 2 Corinthians, see Thomas D. Stegman, *Second Corinthians* (Grand Rapids, MI: Baker Academic, 2009).

4

WHAT IS FORGIVENESS?

Raymond G. Helmick, SJ

When Peter asks, "Lord, if another member of the church sins against me, how often should I forgive him? As many as seven times?" (Matt 18:21). He receives the answer: "Not seven times, but, I tell you, seventy-seven times" (18:22). This is surely not a limiting number, but means: never stop forgiving;, forgive always. And having taught his disciples in their prayer to ask, "...forgive us our debts, as we also have forgiven our debtors" (Matt 6:12). Jesus adds, "For if you forgive others their trespasses, your heavenly Father will also forgive you; but if you do not forgive others, neither will your Father forgive your trespasses" (6:14–15). The universal access to God's forgiveness appears here, but a hint is given also of its limits.

These are characteristic passages of all the Synoptic Gospels —a recurrent theme so closely supplemented by the call for reconciliation (see Matt 5:23–24) that it can be hard to distinguish between them. In Mark 11:25, it reads, "[w]henever you stand praying, forgive, if you have anything against anyone; so that your Father in heaven may also forgive you your trespasses." Luke's version of the Lord's Prayer has, "...forgive us our sins, for we ourselves forgive everyone indebted to us. And do not bring us to the time of trial" (11:4). Jesus himself grants forgiveness unhesitatingly: to the paralytic (Matt 9:6), to those who nailed him to the cross (Luke 23:34).

Jesus, in the Gospels, makes no more insistent demand upon his followers than that they should forgive. That forgiveness has

45

marked Christian life far less in our history can hardly obscure this. Only the demand that our lives be marked by faith or by love can rival the call for forgiveness, and we shall see that these three are closely related, both in terms of present-day world priorities and in their theological meaning. We will need to look at both.

Present Context

In our own time, forgiveness became a lodestone for social scientists and peace activists after the ending of the East/West Cold War. Peace studies were a relatively new phenomenon in the academic world of this period, and with them, the quite secular importance of forgiveness as a way to peace. In the early 1980s, it had seemed a quixotic task to establish what became the United States Institute of Peace under sponsorship of the federal government in Washington. President John F. Kennedy had taken a strong peace line—though along the lines of *si vis pacem, para bellum*—from the beginning of his term. But when he tried to translate this into peaceful compromise in Laos, in Cuba, even in Vietnam, and (after his American University address of June 1963) with the Soviet Union, he ran into massive resistance from the military, intelligence, political, and diplomatic establishments, which some scholars see as the actual reason why he was killed. We were in full Cold War mode, and the Arms Control and Disarmament Agency that Kennedy initiated (a kind of proto-peace establishment) was quickly transformed into the watchdog on Soviet armaments.

Some scholars, like those of Eastern Mennonite University—at that time just training such persons as John Paul Lederach—had grasped the threatening nature of nuclear warfare and were encouraged in their research and field work by Kennedy's success in averting the 1963 Cuban Missile Crisis. But their work remained marginalized until the Cold War began to thaw and came finally to a break in 1989. Interest in forgiveness as part of a broader front of working to win peace and reconciliation—rather than simply achieving victories—stems from this period. Pioneering work had gone before, especially during the 1970s, by Adam Curle—for whom the English Quakers established the first Chair of Peace Studies at Bradford University in 1973, and my own colleague, Austrian Holocaust refugee Richard Hauser. But it was after the end of the Cold War that the academy, psychological and theological, saw that a new agenda had arisen in which forgiveness and reconciliation were understood as the keys to peace.

Major figures in this pursuit were Everett Worthington, Miroslav Volf, and Ervin Staub. From the side of psychology, Worthington's edited book, *Dimensions of Forgiveness: Psychological Research and Theological Perspectives,*[1] brought together the work of many scholars in the field. From a deep theological perspective, Miroslav Volf (Croatian Evangelical theologian), who had experienced the Balkan wars of the 1990s, wrote *Exclusion and Embrace: A Theological Exploration of Identity, Otherness, and Reconciliation* in 1996.[2] Worthington's work as psychologist was joined by that of Ervin Staub, student of altruism and forgiving behavior, who had already been published before the 1980s on the topics of, on the one hand, origins of genocide and, on the other, the roots of positive behavior.[3]

All this interest would be jolted into another sphere after the events of September 11, 2001, when the American public became so virulently infected with its War on Terrorism, and retribution became the national watchword. But a kind of faithful remnant carried on the study of forgiveness despite this new atmosphere of revenge.

In the background of all this interest in a reconciliatory path in conflicts, was the example of Gandhi, celebrated academically and practically in the work of Eugene Sharp, who even in 1973 was publishing his three-volume work, *The Politics of Nonviolent Action,*[4] and was the teacher/trainer of such activists as Lech Walesa in Poland and Mubarak Awad in Palestine. The anti-war stance of Catholic leaders like Thomas Merton and the Berrigan brothers functioned in the context of his nonviolence teaching, and even in the present atmosphere of the Arab Spring in Tunisia and Egypt, the continuing influence of an elderly Gene Sharp can distinctly be seen.[5]

Not all the nonviolence was forgiving, of course, but necessarily forgiveness and reconciliation became hallmarks of a mature, nonviolent strategy. This mark could be seen concretized in the basic strategy of the Mennonite peace strategists, who replaced the term "Conflict Resolution" with "Conflict Transformation." They recognized that, in working with peoples in conflict, it is never possible to fix everything. The objective, instead, should be to transform the relations among people to help them see one another in terms of their full humanity and not simply as "the enemy"; a problem. My visit to Northern Ireland in 1995 illustrated this. I had been asked by friends at Harvard's Conflict Management Center (their title is a term that sounds quite manipulative) to drop their name with people I would be seeing and introduce them as willing to help in the process of reconciliation that, then, occupied everyone's attention. I did so with each of the several Irish Republican Armies (IRAs), with their prisoners at Long Kesh, with the Ulster Defense Association (UDA) and the Ulster Volunteer Force (UVF)—both on the street and in prison, with the British Army, and with the Royal Ultser Constabulary (RUC) and Garda; pretty much all the players. These people were connoisseurs of peace activists, knew who was helpful to them and who was not, and with practical unanimity, spoke of their confidence in John Paul Lederach and Conflict Transformation.

South Africa, at this time, experienced the Truth and Reconciliation Commission (TRC), a movement inspired by Nelson Mandela, Desmond Tutu, and their many colleagues. Reconciliation as the means to peace had already been the message of Mandela in the prison (as it would become that of the various prisoners in Northern Ireland). The TRC, as anyone can narrate now, was not the perfect instrument. It was simply the best anyone had yet done in dealing with a period of national transition after a society's major trauma. Mandela and his colleagues had determined to bring about an amnesty, knowing that a retributive approach to the crimes of apartheid would simply break their society and prevent it from ever healing. This, in fact, was a lesson learned after World War II, when the Allied Powers, mounting their trials at Nuremberg and hanging some of the most prominent offenders, had realized that there would be no German society if they proceeded to hang or imprison all the guilty. Many variations on the hang-them theme or forget-about-the-crimes were played in other transition situations: Argentina and Chile, Poland, East Germany (where the Stasi had kept meticulous files on which spouses and close friends were spying upon whom), and the various other countries of Eastern Europe. The TRC, with a time limit required to get the country in motion again, left many persons' sufferings unaddressed and produced many admissions of guilt that were merely pro forma. But the country was genuinely transformed; not rendered perfect, but made able to breathe and live.

In both Northern Ireland and South Africa, the transformation process took place and was actually initiated by the militant organizations themselves; the bulk of the serious thinking done within the prisons, Robben Island and Long Kesh ("Her Majesty's Prison, the Maze"). These prisoners came to the understanding that they must learn, within their separated communities and traditions, to accommodate one another. That sounded like rather a meager measure of reconciliation, but it was essential. In the Northern Ireland prison, the mantra became that the prisoners and their militant organizations must become the guarantors of one another's differences—accept one another as they are.

In the time since September 11, 2011, when the temperature changed so drastically from forgiveness to vengeance in the American popular culture, the flame has been kept alive. The Templeton Foundation made this a major focus of projects they supported through much of the last two decades, as has the Fetzer Foundation. The Swedish Transitional Foundation has sponsored the work of Charles Harleman, Evelin Lindner, Else Hammerich,

Jan Oberg, Vibeka Vindelov, and others, with their special attention to the devastating traumatic effects of humiliation and their emphasis on human dignity. Their work parallels, in many ways, the studies of violence done at Harvard by James Gilligan, who so commonly finds that the motive for murders in prisons is perceived disrespectful treatment.

The Swedish researchers work in a very secular atmosphere, and that raises again the observation that this work on forgiveness and reconciliation has engaged both theologians and psychologists. Insofar as this happens within the academy, where points are scored by getting articles published, this leads to a certain amount of competition. There is no more fertile ground for turf wars than the academy, and it is commonplace that the other disciplines have a bias to marginalize the theology department. Where the work is at this level, it should not surprise us that the psychology department is interested, for the most part, only in the affective aspects of forgiveness—always important for therapy, especially at the individual level. But that leaves it to the theology department to look into its moral characteristics and inquire about the character-building effects of forgiveness or reconciliation. It is noteworthy, then, that these Swedish scholars, working in their highly secular culture, are fully able to address the value elements of their topics. The same is true, in this country, of either Worthington or Staub.

Integral to the whole enterprise is the work of Restorative Justice, which redefines the legal system, no longer simply as a way to determine guilt and secure the punishment of offenders, but rather to restore relations among persons or peoples. The work of Howard Zehr at Eastern Mennonite University has underlined the close connection between this system of justice and the forgiveness approach to conflicts, as intimate as is the connection with nonviolent forms of protest or resistance to oppression. No system that aims at justice can function as a substitute for accountability. This form of justice must, instead, find ways of compensation and healing that are restorative.

Without these links to nonviolent resistance and restorative justice, the forgiveness and reconciliation movement falls vulnerable to abuse by those defenders of the established order who would like to make it an instrument of submission and a substitute for justice. That tendency becomes especially evident in the Latin countries, where reconciliation and justice demands are often juxtaposed as opposites.

A particular movement in those countries that deserves attention from any proponents of forgiveness is the Fundacion para la Reconciliación, active with its Escuelas de Perdón y Reconciliación in Colombia and several other countries in and beyond Latin American—a work founded by Fr. Leonel Narváez Gómez. With a background working in Kenya, Ethiopia, and Tanzania, Fr. Narváez had become convinced of the necessity of forgiveness as a way of approaching the hardened guerrillas (Left and Right) of his own country and had extended the work of his Foundation to many other conflict situations. This has close affinity with my own practice in many conflicts of approaching always those groups who are most central to the violence of the situation with a supposition that they are not likely simple psychopaths. Rather, they are persons who have undertaken their campaigns for reasons that they believe in, who have seen no other option than force for obtaining some justice they seek (quite possibly misconceived), but who will understand—if they once see convincing alternatives—that their violent course is no longer legitimate. Such persons must be treated with respect, the motivations of their actions sounded, and an understanding sought of what truly stands behind their fears and grievances.

Theological Definition

What, then, do we mean by forgiveness?

The literature can be very stingy in its treatment of forgiveness, more interested in its limits; what we must require before we grant forgiveness, what stipulations must be fulfilled before we grant it. Often, we hear the question of whether we must forget the offense, or the offender, before it can be forgiven. This is an improbable demand, as the offense is truly there before forgiveness can be granted, and to forget or ignore it is rather a method of evasion than of genuine forgiveness. The implication is, then, that the person or the offense cannot truly be forgiven at all, but we can only pretend it is not there.

When have I actually forgiven the other person, group, or community? It can only be when I accept him/her as having uncompromised personal human dignity as a person worthy of love. This does not ignore or deny that I have been offended. The offense is not removed, but it will not be the basis of my attitude toward him/her, of my relation to him/her. This is the beauty of the Mennonite formula; conflict transformation rather than conflict resolution is the objective to be sought in dealing with the relations of people.

Who has not offended? There is theological truth in the proposition that we are all indeed sinners and in need of forgiveness. This is true, not only before God, but before one another. The need for forgiveness is universal at many levels. There are times when I have knowingly offended others/another. There are times I have not even known it or adverted to it, but the offense and the need for forgiveness remains real.

Why, then, should I forgive? The psychologists can tell how much I, in forgiving, am relieved of a burden of unforgiveness. They can trace the workings (physical effects) of forgiveness through the limbic system and prescribe means of therapy. Unquestionably, I will feel better for having forgiven, and can, therefore, do it for my own sake.

Or I may do it for the sake of the other, who stands in need of forgiveness. The question always arises whether or not forgiveness must be a transaction between persons; whether it has to be received and accepted in order really to have happened. That, of course, involves the other person's acknowledgment of the offense—as we say with regard to confessions, it involves repentance and true purpose of amendment. "I forgive you" may in fact be a form of accusation, which the other may want to reject. And it is quite possible that the other person, whom I need to forgive, is not even there, has no awareness of whether I forgive or not, and perhaps, is actually dead. The need for forgiveness remains.

But the true reason for forgiveness is truth. The other truly is a person of full human dignity, deserving of love. That codicil, "deserving of love," may be hard to accept, but it is as God has created the person and how he receives him, despite his (and my) need for forgiveness. It is the truth of our relation to one another.

We may be reluctant also to acknowledge that the other person's human dignity is uncompromised. That amounts to a question of whether an offense is beyond forgiving. Our theological truth, in the light of the Gospel, is that no offense is such.

In all of this, we have to recognize the difficulty and the need for processing. There must be no shortcuts here. My desire, my intention to forgive (difficult to attain in the first place in view of the offense), must not be forced, by myself or through some other's coercion, or it will not be genuine. We may often find such coercion in the attitude that the person who does not forgive (or has not yet forgiven) is somehow morally inferior, and in fact, it is often used by the powerful or those who defend oppression— by themselves or others—as a kind of blackmail over those who have been offended or oppressed. Yet, we must not withdraw the insight that forgiveness of another—a person of human dignity worthy of love—is a work of truth, even if it is a truth we have to work to attain.

This does not remove or contradict my need for caution and to protect myself against future or further hurt. The danger may present itself very manifestly, but that, too, need not define my relation to the other.

How, then, should I combine this with Miroslav Volf's embrace, as a measure of forgiveness? Volf's recommendation, or his demand upon himself, is that we take risks, open ourselves to the other (even the dangerous other) in welcome to his humanity.[6] This brings the action of forgiveness beyond attitude and into concrete action (even heroic action), and can, therefore, not be made a demand on anyone other than oneself. But it is a path, doubtless an extreme path, that makes forgiveness into something practical. Volf describes it in terms of the actual process of embrace: opening one's arms in welcome to the other, which makes one vulnerable if the other should choose to attack, rejecting the offer; closing one's arms about the other, which unites us in the embrace but also disables the other in his ability to attack; letting go again, so that the other remains free; and standing, then, in acceptance of the other as a sign of the reconciliation that one hopes will come of the forgiveness.[7]

All this is figurative language, which will mean many different courses of action in particular circumstances, but always involves that choice of vulnerability in the presence of the other. If that cannot be demanded of any other than oneself, it is also a means to draw actual consequences from the act of forgiveness; heroic, indeed, but the true cost of forgiveness.

Forgiveness, as described here, does not present easy options. It forms one of the more difficult practices in the following of Christ but is entirely integral to it. The example of Jesus, in making himself entirely vulnerable to those who would do him ill and ultimately accepting death at their hands, for their sake as well as for any and all others, beckons to the actually heroic stance, beyond what can be demanded of anyone by others, but a measure of commitment in the one who will exercise it. Unmistakably, it is also the manifestation of the love of enemies of whom Jesus speaks and a way to restore relations with that offending or dangerous other, bringing about peace.

Notes

1. Everett L. Worthington Jr., ed. *Dimensions of Forgiveness: Psychological Research and Theological Perspectives* (Philadelphia, PA: Templeton Foundation Press, 1998).

2. Miroslav Volf, *Exclusion and Embrace: A Theological Exploration of Identity, Otherness, and Reconciliation* (Nashville, TN: Abingdon Press, 1996).

3. See *Positive Social Behavior and Morality*, vol. 1, *Personal and Social Influences* (New York: Academic Press, 1978); vol. 2, *Socialization and Development* (New York: Academic Press, 1979); Ervin Staub and Daniel Bar-Tal, eds. *Development and Maintenance of Prosocial Behavior: International Perspectives on Positive Morality* (New York: Plenum Press, 1984); Ervin Staub, *The Roots of Evil: The Origins of Genocide and Other Group Violence* (New York: Cambridge University Press, 1989); Nancy Eisenberg and Ervin Staub, eds. *Social and Moral Values: Individual and Societal Perspectives* (Hillsdale, NJ: Larry Erlbaum Associates, 1989); and Daniel Bar-Tal and Ervin Staub, eds. *Patriotism in the Lives of Individuals and Nations* (Chicago, IL: Nelson-Hall Publications, 1997).

4. *The Politics of Nonviolent Action*, 3 vols. (Boston, MA: Porter Sargent, 1973).

5. See Gene Sharp's more recent books: *From Dictatorship to Democracy: A Conceptual Framework for Liberation* (Boston, MA: The Albert Einstein Institution, 2003); *Waging Nonviolent Struggle: 20th Century Practice and 21st Century Potential* (Boston, MA: Extending Horizons Books, 2005).

6. Volf, *Exclusion and Embrace*.

7. Ibid.

5

JUSTICE MATTERS! THEOLOGY AND A RELATIONAL, RESTORATIVE JUSTICE

Thomas W. Porter

Reconciliation Involves Justice, Right Relations

Relationships are not simple, easy, "perfect," or free of conflict, but life is about relationships where we find our greatest joy and fulfillment. Healing and reconciling broken relationships is a journey that is hard, challenging, and involves risks, but this is a journey to which we are called, a journey where we travel on sacred ground.

Reconciliation describes the work of God in this world, in history. God is a covenant-making God, who is constantly drawing creation back to faithful relation in the covenant. Reconciliation is also our calling, our work as well (2 Cor 5:17–20). This reconciliation is not about "cheap" reconciliation with God and with our neighbor. Reconciliation is a movement toward right relations, just relationships. Justice matters in any discussion of reconciliation. Justice is more important to God than worship (Amos 5:21–24). The worth of worship is contingent upon being just and righteous in one's relationships, fulfilling the obligations of relationships. Our understanding of justice matters. Our misunderstanding of justice can distort our understanding of God, our understanding of God's atoning work, and our practice of justice. I want to explore my experience with justice as a trial lawyer, minister, mediator, and teacher, and how it informs my understanding of theology, God's work of atonement, and the practice.

A Trial Lawyer's Story

Let me begin with a story from my first day of practice as a trial lawyer. I arrived to discover that the partner for whom I was working had just started a long trial. He left me a tape, describing the work that he wanted me to do. He also took the time to give me his wisdom about the trial practice, about trying cases. He concluded by giving me a description of the other partners in the firm and their particular styles. I remember two of the descriptions. The first was a Catholic partner, a deeply religious man who went to Mass every morning. He described him as a pugilist. In cross-examination of adverse witnesses, he would come out swinging. The witnesses would see the blows coming, but there was nothing they could do about it. He left them a bloody pulp. The second was a Quaker, the greatest gentleman he had ever known, soft-spoken and kind. In cross-examination of adverse witnesses, he used a different approach. He used a stiletto. The witnesses would generally never see it coming. Sometimes they would not feel it going between the ribs, but the result was the same, a pool of blood under the witness chair.

I experienced different reactions to this story. The first was amusement, a Quaker with a stiletto, and then dismay. I began to say to myself that I would be neither. I was also a minister and saw myself wanting to be like Atticus Finch, the gentleman lawyer in *To Kill a Mockingbird*.[1] It took me a long time to understand the full import of this story. No image or metaphor captures the whole of my litigation practice, but as I began to try cases, I found that I became skilled with a stiletto. My boss was just being honest. A system of zealous advocacy and retributive justice not only can cause a Quaker to use a stiletto, but a United Methodist minister/lawyer to do the same.

As I continued to try cases over the course of twenty five years, a lover's quarrel with the practice became more intense. My problem was not with the rule of law and with due process. I have a deep regard for human rights, which I see as a source of empowerment, important to protecting us as individuals and also as a source of right relations in community, binding us together in mutual responsibility and obligation. Just talking with my two teaching assistants over the last year, one from Zimbabwe and one from the Congo, has confirmed again the importance of the rule of law, the protection of basic human rights, and the role of lawyers independent of the state. My problem is not with lawyers as advocates. I don't know any role nobler than standing up for fellow human beings and helping tell their story. My problem was with aspects of the adversarial-retributive system of justice. Everyone is familiar with the adversarial approach to justice. We see it in television dramas and in movies that depict lawyers as combatants, fighting it out in the courtroom. Retributive justice is the justice that asks two questions: did you do it, and if so, how should you be punished? This is the justice of an eye for an eye.

One of the interesting things that happened to me is that I discovered this system of the courtroom influencing the way we dealt with conflict and harm in other arenas. As the lawyer for the United Methodist churches in New England for twenty three years, I saw it in the way we dealt with grievances against ministers in our church trials. As a mediator, working for the JustPeace Center for Mediation and Conflict Transformation in the United Methodist Church, I saw it in church disputes, which are often very adversarial and retributive. As a citizen and teacher of conflict transformation and peace building, I saw it in the way groups of people deal with each other, like the Israelis and the Palestinians, for example. As a theologian, I saw it even in the dominant understanding of the atonement.

Before I describe my quarrel with the adversarial-retributive system, I do want to affirm the basic moral principle of retributive justice: this is a moral universe. Wrongs need to receive moral condemnation, and we need to be accountable for our actions when we do harm. We need to treat human beings as moral persons who take responsibility for what they do. This is important to affirming the dignity and freedom of individuals. I just think that there is a better way to deal with accountability in most cases than coerced accountability in the form of punishment. I recognize that we need an adversarial system to deal with false accusation and/or entrenched denial of wrongdoing. Some cases need to be tried for precedent-setting purposes and when they cannot be resolved by those with a direct stake in the offense. For me, such an adversarial system is a system of last resort. There are collaborative ways of dealing with most cases of harm in this world, as evidenced by the growth of the mediation movement and the "vanishing trial." Even when guilt is established by a court, there is still the possibility of sentencing through a restorative justice process.

Problems with the Adversarial-Retributive System

Increased Relational Animosity and Estrangement

Coerced retributive justice requires an adversarial process. Having tried many cases over twenty five years, I do not remember a case where the parties left the courtroom feeling closer to each other. In fact, I generally found their relationship more strained than ever. Now I am sure there are exceptions to this observation, but I do know that the system is not conducive to healing relationships. I believe that relational healing in this world is what God wants and what we need. Such relational healing ideally involves a journey of apology, making things right for offenders and forgiveness for victims, and reconciliation for both in the creation of a new relation. The adversarial-retributive system does not open space for such a journey, a space conducive to overcoming social distance. It does not provide opportunities for empathy and recognition of the other. Instead, it creates a space for combat. It is about winning. Lawsuits almost always exacerbate anger, wounds, divisions, greed, and a desire for revenge. The process can deepen societal wounds and conflict.

Lack of Focus and Care for Victims and the Harm Experienced

The criminal justice system in the United States is offender focused. The question is whether the defendant broke the law, and, if so, what the punishment should be. The victim is often victimized twice, once by the crime and then by the process, including cross-examination. The state is seen in this system as the party that has been harmed, but the state is not the primary victim. Yes, there have been attempts in recent history to give more of a role to the victim than just being a witness for the prosecution, but limited things can be done in a system focused on the offender. The primary victim's harm should be personally addressed, as well as the harm to society as a whole.

The Focus on Punishment and the Lack Thereof on Real Accountability for Offenders

Punishment involves the infliction of pain. This might be the deprivation of something valued, for example, freedom, money, or life. Punishment is inflicted as a response to the determination of a violation of the law and in a way that somehow corresponds to the offense.

Conrad Brunk, a philosopher of law, says, "But retributive theory has never been able to give a plausible account of how the infliction of harm or deprivation of liberty amounts to *taking responsibility*. Even less has it been able to explain how it rights the wrong or restores justice, which it claims to do."[2] Brunk also says, "Because of retributivism's preoccupation with infliction of harm

60

as the means by which wrongs are made right, it simply blinds itself to the fact that the real injustice of an offense is the loss and harm suffered by the *victims*. This injustice is not addressed by the suffering of the offender—the loss is not restored, the suffering is not compensated, the broken relationships with victims and society are not mended. The injustice remains."[3]

Coerced accountability is not real accountability. Real accountability is when the offender personally takes responsibility for the harm and does something to make things right. This is the accountability that can make a difference to the victim and to the offender. My experience is that most people in prison see themselves as victims (in many ways they are) and have not taken responsibility for their actions. Without such personal accountability, offenders do not change their patterns of behavior for the better. A punishment system aimed at inflicting pain is not the best way to encourage personal accountability. As George Bernard Shaw says, "If you are to punish a man retributively you must injure him. If you are to reform him, you must improve him. And men are not improved by injuries."[4] A punishment system discourages offenders from empathizing with victims, acknowledging their responsibility, and addressing the harm created by their action. Offenders create rationalizations of their behavior and stereotypes of their victims. As Howard Zehr says, "They come to believe that what they did was not too serious, that the victim 'deserved' it, that everyone is doing it, that insurance will take care of any losses. They find ways to divert blame from themselves to other people and situations. They also employ stereotypes about victims and potential victims. Unconsciously or even consciously they work to insulate themselves from the victim."[5] We need a system that encourages personal, real accountability for the sake of the victim and the offender as well as for society as a whole.

Finally, I agree with Christopher Marshall, a New Testament professor from New Zealand, when he says, "Social civility and public safety are diminished, not enhanced, when societies become increasingly acclimatized to regimes of harsh punishment, such as imprisonment. Far from deterring crime, prison fosters the corrupt and violent behavior it purports to control, then returns it to the streets when prisoners are released. A vicious cycle is set up in which crime demands punishment, punishment entrenches crime, and continuing crime demands yet more and more punishment."[6]

A Need for Seeing the Individual in Context

Yes, we need to affirm personal responsibility, but we need to see the individual in context as well. The adversarial-retributive system, in general, sees the alleged offender as an isolated unit in society and solely in terms of personal free will. Life is more complex and relational. Life is interconnected and interdependent. Most offenders have been victims in one way or another. Many have been abused as children. James Gilligan, New York University professor and former prison psychiatrist, says, "The emotion of shame is the primary or ultimate cause of all violence, whether toward others or toward the self."[7] My experience is that trials just exacerbate this shame. They do nothing to address this shame. Crime does involve a social context. The offender is more than just the act of the alleged crime. For the offender's sake and possible transformation into a good citizen, and for our sake in trying to create a safer, less harmful community, we need to provide a space and a system where we can more fully understand the context of the offender.

Barriers to Truth-Telling

Truth often loses in this system. My experience with the adversarial-retributive system is that its emphasis on winning, with painful consequences for losing, creates an atmosphere for lying, denial, and self-justification. John Henry Wigmore, who wrote an influential book on evidence in the American judicial system, believed that cross-examination was the greatest engine for truth telling ever invented. Several judge friends have said to me that this simply is not true. What they have observed is that cross-examination is one of the best forms of manipulation ever invented.

No Real Engagement of the Parties

The adversarial-retributive system does not allow the parties to dialogue or talk with each other. Christopher Marshall articulates well the need for engagement of the parties: "Because they are bound together to the event, both victim and offender need each other to experience the liberation and healing from the continuing thrall of the offense. The offender needs the victim to trigger or sharpen his contrition, to hear his confession, remit his guilt, and to affirm his ability to start fresh. The victim needs the offender to hear her pain, answer her questions, absorb her resentment, and affirm her dignity. Each holds the key to the other's liberation."[8] Friends, for example, who are part of Murder Victim's Families for Reconciliation have told me that this is true. The system, as we know it, does not create space and a forum for such engagement. Lawyers tell their clients not to speak to the opposing party. In fact, most defense attorneys in criminal cases do not allow their clients to testify. We need to create spaces that are conducive to overcoming social distance and to encourage real engagement and dialogue.

No Real Opportunity for the Community to Address the Social Causes of Harm

Kay Pranis, Judge Barry Stuart, and Mark Wedge have argued that when the state takes over in our name, it undermines our sense of community and our sense of responsibility for the health and welfare of our communities, which includes a concern for victims and offenders, as well as the need to address the root causes of crime.[9] Juries are limited in what they can do. They act to determine guilt and punishment. There is no opportunity given them as representatives of the community to address the underlying social context for the crime. They cannot address issues such as: What are the obligations of the community? What can we do to make such crimes less likely? How can we make our community safer and healthier? This is not to say that there is no place for the state. The state, through legislators and courts, creates our laws; through the police, provides for public safety and for the investigation of crimes; and through our courts, provides the forum of last resort. It does say that the state can and should make room for and support practices of restorative justice.

Negative Effects on Clients and Practitioners

All too often, people come away from the process wounded, including the practitioners. The goal is to win, but many people come away from litigation feeling that everyone has lost, with the lawyers being the only ones who benefited, at least financially, from the process. I have talked with many practitioners who feel dehumanized by the system. We need to care about lawyers and their spiritual health and well-being as well as for our clients.

Search for an Alternative to the Adversarial-Retributive System

My quarrel with the adversarial-retributive system led me to search for a better way. This journey first led me from the courtroom to tables of conversation, dialogue, and mediation, finding an alternative to the adversarial nature of the system. In the mid-90s, I was able to study mediation at Harvard Law School and later at Eastern Mennonite University. As a mediator, I learned to engage conflict and address harm by working toward restructuring relationships and empowering participants to solve their own problems and transform their conflicts. I will never forget the feeling after I facilitated my first mediation. It was truly a spiritual experience. I felt that I had found my authentic self, free to be empathetic and compassionate to both parties. I marveled at the parties' ability to resolve their own conflicts and to come to a better place in their relationship.

In mediation, I found an alternative to the adversarial nature of the system, but I was still searching for an alternative to retributive justice. What is the justice that serves collaboration? My search took me to South Africa, where I studied the Truth and Reconciliation Commission (TRC). In South Africa, I felt as if I had "come home." Here, an understanding of the relational nature of life came alive through the African concept of *ubuntu*: we are who we are because of our relationships. When I dehumanize you, I dehumanize myself. We are interconnected and interdependent with one another and with the whole web of life. Life is about relationships! I saw the power in telling and hearing each other's stories. I witnessed the essential practice of forgiveness. I also discovered a new understanding of justice, restorative justice. Critics of the TRC asked, "Where is justice?" "Where are the adversarial retributive trials such as were experienced at Nuremberg after World War II in Germany?" I listened to Bishop Tutu agree that retributive justice was not the justice they were seeking. There was another form of justice, restorative justice, which was consistent with the desire to seek truth and reconciliation. The final clause on National Unity and Reconciliation in the Interim Constitution of 1993 says this well:

> The pursuit of national unity, the well-being of all South African citizens and peace require reconciliation between the people of South Africa and the reconstruction of society...there is a need for understanding but not revenge, a need for reparation but not for retaliation, a need for *ubuntu* but not for victimization.

Upon my return from South Africa, I studied with Howard Zehr at Eastern Mennonite University, who taught me that this justice moves us from a narrow focus on punishing offenders to "a process to involve, to the extent possible, those who have a stake in a specific offense and to collectively identify and address harms, needs, and obligations, in order to heal and put things as right as possible."[10] Much of what I say about restorative justice I learned from Zehr, often called the father of the modern-day restorative justice movement. Since the late 90s, I have been trying to practice restorative justice, primarily in grievance procedures in the United Methodist Church, dealing with cases such as embezzlement and sexual abuse. I have been impressed with how restorative justice has found resonance in places such as the board of the *Journal of Law and Religion*, with which I have been associated for more than twenty-five years.

Restorative Justice

In this paper, I will not be able to do justice to restorative justice, but I can present some of its basic principles and show how it responds to my concerns with adversarial-retributive justice. These principles are what connects us with our theology, our understanding of God's atoning work, and the practices that open up the possibility of doing justice.

Restorative justice is a relatively new movement. However, the history of its principles are deeply imbedded in traditional systems, including systems that were in place in the West before states decided that they would be more powerful if they took over community justice systems. It has been largely a grass-roots movement that has become influential internationally. The movement is in many ways still at a formative stage. Much still needs to be learned, studied, and practiced. In dealing with conflicted relationships that have experienced harm, there is no simple, easy, pain free, perfect way to work together to come to a healing place. This is hard work. It is not about perfection. It takes time. It involves risk, including the risk of failure. I do find, however, that restorative justice does respond in a good way to my concerns with the present system.

Relational Justice: Crime is a Violation of People and Interpersonal Relations

Restorative justice is an attempt to ground justice in the reality described by *ubuntu*. We are interconnected and interdependent. As modern science—especially the field of neuroscience—is discovering, we are "hardwired" for relationship. As human beings, we do want to be connected in a good way. Crime is seen "as a wound in the community, a tear in the web of relationships."[11] Restorative justice calls us to focus on the relationships between victims, offenders, and the community, always remembering that each participant and relationship is unique, honoring the dignity of each participant and showing mutual respect. Restorative justice and its practices allow for a space where relationships can be addressed and, ideally, recreated in a good way where individuals can flourish.

This does not mean that we ignore the law, whether it is created by legislators, courts, or contracts. Law, for me, is primarily society's description of the minimal obligations for just relations, for example, the relation between a landlord and a tenant or a product manufacturer and a consumer. The law is an important guide to the relational life. We know laws can be unjust, but, ideally, law is a positive force in defining, encouraging, and improving our social relations. Both human rights and the law are important boundaries for persons in relation. In restorative justice, we begin to have a greater understanding of the relational context and purpose of the law and how law helps us understand the harm experienced. Relationships, however, are always greater than the sum of their parts. The obligations of relationships are always greater than the minimal obligations of the law. In practices of restorative justice, we are given the opportunity to understand the legal obligations of relationships as well as the obligations that are personal and contextual to a specific relationship, as we recreate, re-weave, re-story relationships so they are more just.

A Focus on Harm, the Harm Experienced by Victims

If crime is a violation of people, not just the state, then we must look at who has been harmed and how they have been harmed. For restorative justice, we must start with the direct victims of the wrongful act. This means hearing from the victim how they have been harmed and what they feel needs to be done to redress the harm. These needs are those needs expressed by the victims, not some script for victims. These needs are evaluated in light of the law, as described above, and in light of the obligations of the relationship. Restorative justice is victim oriented, but not victim controlled as the redress is determined through a process of dialogue with the offender and other important stakeholders.

In many cases, we find ourselves as both victims and offenders, and restorative process opens up the possibility of understanding the reality of this truth, not just producing a winner and a loser. Everyone's needs are different, but there are some needs that are mentioned over and over again as I have listened to parties to a wrongdoing. Briefly, victimization leads to disorder, disempowerment, and disconnection. The journey toward healing involves finding order, empowerment, and new relational connections. Finding order involves *safety*. The person harmed ideally needs to know that he or she will not be harmed again. Finding empowerment involves *being heard* (telling the story without interruption with all the feelings, in a space where people truly listen, understand, and acknowledge the harm), *receiving answers* (What really happened? Why me? Why you? What has happened since?), *vindication* through restitution and accountability, and *participation* in the conversation, including what needs to be done to address the harm. Finding new relational connections involves a journey of *healing*. My experience is that restorative justice processes can address these needs in ways that are not generally possible in an adversarial-retributive process.

Real Accountability

Restorative justice agrees with the moral principle behind retributive justice. Offenders need to be treated as morally responsible citizens and be held accountable for their wrongdoing. For restorative justice, this means that the offender addresses the needs of the person who was harmed. These needs create obligations. Personal accountability means that offenders actually do things, both concretely and symbolically, that attempt to make things right, to repair the harm. This includes restitution but also other actions of taking responsibility such as remorse and apology. Real accountability addresses the harm done to the community as well. Taking accountability for one's actions is an important step in being reintegrated into the community. Yes, addressing the needs of the victim by taking responsibility for one's actions can be a much harder journey than receiving the punishment of the state. It can involve pain and suffering, but it is a different kind of pain, pain that signals a transformation of the person. A restorative justice process can also, at the same time, understand and address the fuller context of the offender, including unresolved trauma, shame, or harm, and the offender's need to be reintegrated in the life of the community. This journey will often involve treatment and sometimes restraint.

Engagement

Restorative justice attempts to engage all the parties in the process. This is a collaborative engagement. This is where the principles of the mediation movement come together with the principles of restorative justice. The ideal is to have an actual dialogue between the parties as occurs in victim–offender conferencing, circles of accountability, and healing and family group conferences. Here, all the parties share their stories, listen to each other, seek to understand each other, and work to come to consensus on what should be done. Such actual engagement is not always possible or culturally appropriate, and creative ways have been developed to exchange information and to involve everyone in the decision-making process, even when all the parties are not able to meet in the same room. My experience in such engagements is that there is much more truth telling, as the parties speak directly to each other as well as to others from their families and communities who are significant to them. The dialogue is not a manipulated cross-examination. Remarkable things can happen as social distance is overcome, stories are told, and needs are described; persons begin to hear each other, and parties work together to determine real accountability and find a measure of healing in the process.

The Community Is Involved

People from the community are often involved to help provide a space safe enough where victims and offenders can come together and tell their stories. They can help victims express their needs and offenders to meet their obligations, as well as work toward the healing and reintegration of both. They can also, unlike a jury, work to discern the root causes of the wrongdoing and express ideas on how the community might respond. Victims find it helpful, in my experience, to hear that something is being done to make it less likely that anyone else will be injured as they were. Much work needs to be done by advocates of restorative justice on defining community and involving communities of care. The key questions according to Zehr are: "1) who in the community cares about these people or about this offense, and 2) how can we involve them in the process."[12] Ultimately, restorative justice is about building community.

Restorative Justice and God's Atoning, Reconciling Work

Where do the principles of restorative justice find resonance in theology, and how does an understanding of biblical theology support and deepen the understanding and practice of restorative justice? Here I am, speaking out of my own faith tradition as a Christian. I have learned much about restorative justice from my Jewish and Muslim friends, for example.

Restoration of the Covenantal Relation: God's Justice

God, in the Bible, is seen as a covenant-creating and covenant-maintaining God. The sum of the law and the prophets is to love God, love the neighbor, and love the self, with all three being important, balancing individual self worth, creative freedom, and the dignity of difference with social responsibility and the experience of the unity of all creation (Mark 12:30–31). As Martin Buber said, "In the beginning is the Relation."[13] God is a relational God who creates and sustains relationships. God's goal for creation is *shalom*, right relations and well being within these relationships. Biblical justice is about relationships. God's justice within the covenant is seen as the fulfillment of the obligations of the relationship, and God calls us to practice the same justice by fulfilling our relational obligations.[14] God is always faithful to the covenant. God's creation is not always faithful, and God's action in history is to restore the created order to the covenant, to right relations, just relations within the covenant. For Christians, God's restoring, reconciling work is seen in the life, death, and resurrection of Jesus, in whom we believe God was fully present. As Paul said, "All this is from God, who reconciled us to himself through Christ, and has given us the ministry of reconciliation…" (2 Cor 5:18).

Solidarity with Victims

God's solidarity with those who have experienced oppression or harm in life is seen in the two principle stories in the Bible, the Exodus from Egypt and the life, death, and resurrection of Jesus. We hear over and over again in the Bible that God sides with the least, the orphan, the widow, the poor, the oppressed, the people who have experienced injustice. Jesus, on the cross, was an innocent victim. Jesus was punished, but not by God. He experienced, in his body, all the injustice and violence of these systems. He even experienced the deepest despair we can experience; feeling abandoned, abandoned by the only One who can truly give us hope. Believing that God was incarnate in Jesus, we see that God experienced this sense of abandonment, fully experiencing solidarity with human suffering. God is with us. In Matthew 18, which is the most practical advice Jesus gave us for dealing with harm, we see Jesus starting with victims, the ones who have been sinned against. He says they have the moral authority to go directly to and confront the person who harmed them. If the offender does not listen, then the victim can take witnesses along to assist. If the offender still does not listen, the victim can tell it to the church; the whole body working to help the parties listen and respond in a good way to each other. In the Bible, listening is more than hearing and understanding. It is seen in a response that works to make things right.

Andrew Sung Park's understanding of the Korean concept of *han* has been helpful to me in understanding this solidarity with victims. He describes *han* as "a deep, unhealed wound of a victim that festers in her or him. It can be a social, economic, political, physical, mental or spiritual wound generated by political oppression, economic exploitation, social alienation, cultural contempt, injustice, poverty or war."[15] Jesus came not just for sinners but also to liberate victims of injustice, heal them from their *han*. For Park, "Jesus' blood was not shed to pay human debts to God; rather, it was shed to restore the integrity of victims through God's justice and compassion. Jesus came not to appease God's wrath but to manifest God's intention to restore humanity...Jesus came to vindicate suffering victims and to restore their human dignity."[16] On the cross, Jesus brought liberation to victims and salvation to offenders.

Forgiveness of Offenders

Jesus confronted offenders, exposing their violence and injustice, and offered them forgiveness. Yes, there is much retributive justice in the Bible, but not in the life and teachings of Jesus. We see that the grand arc of the Bible is from the law of Lamech in Genesis 4:24, unlimited revenge ("seventy-seven fold"); to limited retribution (an eye for an eye), a great advance in responding to harm; to unlimited forgiveness ("seventy-seven times") in Matthew 18:22. In Matthew 5:38–42, Jesus rejects an eye for an eye and gives us a new, non-violent way of responding. We hear the word of forgiveness from the cross. Jesus named evil wherever he saw it and resisted evil in all its forms. He also understood that you can't fight evil on its own terms—with violence. He realized that you can't fight evil by becoming what you hate.[17] A way to break the spiral of violence and retribution in this life is through the journey to forgiveness. The way to reconciliation—to loving the enemy—is through forgiveness. The judgment on the cross was the judgment of love, which is more convicting than any punishment.

Accountability

Jesus tell us in Matthew 18:3 that if we don't accept accountability for our actions through confession, repentance, and actions to make things right, we will not enter the Kingdom or experience *shalom*. The Kingdom door is always open, but, if we do not see our wrongdoing and work to make things right, we will not have the vision, the heart, and the spirit to see the door, to walk through it, and to receive the forgiveness that has been offered. Accountability in Matthew 18 is not an imposed or coerced accountability. The reality is that if we do not accept accountability, the cycles of violence and retribution will continue.

Retributive Theories of the Atonement

Restorative Justice and our understanding of biblical justice liberate us from retributive views of God and God's atonement. At the heart of Anslem's satisfaction theory[18] and Calvin's penal substitution theory,[19] together often called the blood-atonement theory, is an assumption that God's justice is retributive. Jesus must die to satisfy the honor or the justice of God. There is no way out except for the sacrifice of God's son. To satisfy such a justice, there needs to be an eye for eye, a punishment so that sin does not go unchecked and unpunished. However, God did not kill Jesus as a sacrificial substitute for our sins. As Abelard, a young contemporary of Anselm said, "Indeed, how cruel and wicked it seems that anyone should demand the blood of the innocent person as the price for anything, or that it should in any way please him that an innocent man should be slain—still less that God should consider the death of his Son so agreeable that by it he should be reconciled to the whole world."[20] As many women theologians have noted, God is not a child abuser. God's justice is restorative, not retributive. Jesus did not die to satisfy God's retributive justice but to express God's restorative justice. This does not mean that our sins have no consequences to God and to God's creation. God always stands against evil and injustice. God's way of restoring is not to punish Jesus as a substitute, but to break the cycles of punishment, violence, and retribution through solidarity with us as victims and forgiveness to us as offenders, who receive this forgiveness through repentance, a real accountability.

From my experience in dealing with retributive justice in the courts and a retributive way of dealing with disagreements and conflicts in all arenas of life, I believe that it is important to know that this is not the way God works, the way God created the universe. Christopher Marshall documents how "the identification of divine righteousness with God's vindictive or punitive justice" has distorted our thinking about justice. When we fail to realize that justification is restorative and not retributive, according to

Marshall, we often separate justification from issues of social justice, and good works are seen as a direct threat to the idea of justification by grace and not by works.[21] Tim Gorringe documents the deleterious influence of the belief that God punished Jesus retributively for the sins of the world in defense of his own holiness. Gorringe demonstrates that harsh punishment increased in societies that adopted this view of the atonement. If we believe that God is retributive, which these views of the atonement express, and we believe in imitating God or find this as justification for our own actions, we are more likely to be retributive.[22] What came first? My sense is that our retributive views of God are projections of our own human response to wrongdoing, based largely in the reptilian brain, which originally helped us survive. Durkheim said that the appeal of the penal theory of the atonement lies in the human desire for revenge, masquerading behind a concern for the honor of the deity.[23] I also sense that these projections, then, were mirrored back, giving our retributive instincts divine sanction. My other observation is that the Christian communities that believe most strongly in the atonement theories based on God's justice as retributive are those who are also strongest in support of military solutions to our problems. Connected with this is the myth that violence saves, the strongest and most powerful myth in the world today, according to Walter Wink.[24] A retributivist view of the cross includes sacred violence. I also see these atonement theories as responsible, in part, for the loss of focus on God's reconciling acts and on the call to be ministers of reconciliation.

God's Restorative Justice at the Table of Holy Communion

For me, the most important place where Christians are going to overcome tendencies toward retribution and punishment and find God's atoning work most fully expressed is at the Table of

Holy Communion.[25] This is the Table where we are formed into peacebuilders, into reconcilers. At this Table, we see that we are interconnected and interdependent, needing each other. We are told that God stands in solidarity with us when we are harmed and that we are loved and forgiven in spite of our ongoing breaches of the covenant with God and neighbor. We learn that the only way we are going to break out of the cycles of retribution and violence that are tearing our world and our relationships apart is through forgiveness. The Table is a place of accountability to God, to each other, to the cosmos. It is a table of restorative justice, of healing. We pass the peace, recognizing that we are called to be practitioners of restorative justice and reconciliation.

The most important lesson we learn at this Table comes when we remember the night when Jesus had his last supper with his disciples. The first thing he does in Mark is name the conflict in the room: "one of you will betray me" (Mark 14:17–20). In John, he also names the whole conflictual system of his day by moving from the head of the table to the foot of the table, taking the place of the least, and washes the feet of all the disciples (John 13:3–17). Here, Jesus taught us the importance of naming the harm, naming the sin, naming the evil. Truth requires it. Justice requires it. Transformation requires it.

What Jesus does next is remarkable, radical, and transforming in the context of his day and ours. Jesus names the conflict, but not in order to give a stone or to set the stage for retribution and punishment. He names it and then gives bread and wine. Indeed, he gives his life. When the second step in the process after naming is giving bread, the tone of the naming is changed. It does not have the tone of blaming or humiliation. It does not have the "feel" of a statement to punish or wound or humiliate or dismiss. It creates a difference in the speaker and in the hearer. It opens up a different spirit in the speaker. It opens up, in the hearer, in large part because of this different spirit, the possibility of openness to real accountability as opposed to a purely defensive response. There is a judgment here, but it is the judgment of love.

The frame within which Jesus calls us to live out our lives is not the frame of naming to punish, but the frame of naming to give bread. At this Table, I find the fullest response to my search for a better way than the adversarial–retributive model. Here we move from blaming to naming, from punishment to accountability, from retribution to forgiveness. I know that "giving bread" can include many generative possibilities and that moving from the initial desire to give a stone to giving bread is a journey for us human beings. It is a journey that cannot be mandated or coerced. It is a journey that is different for each of us.

The giving of bread does not negate the reality that our deeds have consequences, that accountability is important. Jesus says at the Last Supper, "For the Son of Man goes as it is written of him, but woe to that one by whom the Son of Man is betrayed! It would have been better for that one not to have been born" (Mark 14:21). We read in Matthew that Judas recognized his sin, threw down the pieces of silver in the Temple, and hanged himself (Matt 27:3–5). There are consequences for our actions. However, none of this is seen here as God's or Jesus' retribution against Judas. The hanging is self-imposed. The naming and the giving of bread have the potential of making all things new.

I believe this Table, with this framing of our worldview, is the place we will understand that in the life, death, and resurrection of Jesus, we were freed from the cycles of violence and retribution, and we no longer need to believe that violence will save us or that justice is achieved through retribution. At this Table, we will understand that God's atoning work is restorative, and we will be formed into reconcilers who practice a relational, restorative justice.

Conclusion

Justice matters! Theology matters! How does this "naming to give bread" work in this world of relational complexity and deep relational brokenness—a world where the "powers" that do harm and are destructive of the relational life are strong and pervasive? With courage and humility! With no illusions but with hope! With creativity and imagination! With knowledge that we are not alone! With a sense that we're always working on a spectrum from retribution to restoration, taking actions that might be partially restorative, realizing that we need to celebrate each advance toward restoration, and always working for the fullest experience of restorative justice we can achieve. With careful preparation, creating spaces where people can tell their stories and dialogue with each other about harm and accountability, and being surprised by the miracle of healing that can occur.

Notes

1. This is a book by Harper Lee about Atticus Finch defending an African American unjustly accused of a murder. Atticus Finch has been the subject of books written about the gentleman lawyer.

2. Conrad Brunk, "Restorative Justice and the Philosophical Theories of Criminal Punishment," in *The Spiritual Roots of Restorative Justice*, ed. Michael L. Hadley (Albany: State University of New York Press, 2001), 48.

3. Ibid., 38.

4. Christopher Marshall, *Beyond Retribution: A New Testament Vision for Justice, Crime and Punishment* (Grand Rapids, MI: Eerdmans, 2001), 102–3.

5. Howard Zehr, *Changing Lenses: A New Focus for Crime and Justice* (Scottdale, PA: Herald Press, 1990), 40–41.

6. Marshall, *Beyond Retribution,* 107.

7. James Gilligan, *Violence, Reflections on a National Epidemic* (New York: Vintage Books, 1996), 119.

8. Marshall, *Beyond Retribution,* 277.

9. Kay Pranis, Barry Stuart, Mark Wedge, *Peacemaking Circles: From Crime to Community* (St. Paul, MN: Living Justice Press, 2003), 13–14.

10. Howard Zehr, *The Little Book of Restorative Justice* (Intercourse, PA: Good Books, 2002), 37.

11. Ibid., 20.

12. Ibid., 28.

13. Martin Buber, *I and Thou*, trans. Walter Kaufmann (New York: Charles Scribner's Sons, 1970), 69.

14. E. R. Achtemeier, "Righteousness in the Old Testament" in *The Interpreter's Dictionary of the Bible* (New York: Abingdon Press, 1962), 4:80.

15. Andrew Sung Park, *Triune Atonement: Christ's Healing for Sinners, Victims, and the Whole Creation* (Louisville, KY: Westminster John Knox Press, 2009), 39.

16. Ibid., 70–71.

17. See Walter Wink, *Engaging the Powers: Discernment and Resistance in a World of Domination* (Minneapolis: Fortress Press, 1992).

18. Anselm, *Cur Deus Homo*, in *Anselm of Canterbury*, trans. and ed. Jasper Hopkins and Herbert Richardson (Toronto and New York: Edwin Mellen Press, 1974), 102.

19. John Calvin, *Institutes of the Christian Religion*, ed. John T. McNeill, trans. Ford Lewis Battles (Philadelphia: Westminster Press, 1960), 2.16.2.

20. Peter Abelard, *Exposition of the Epistle to the Romans*, excerpted in *A Scholastic Miscellany: Anselm to Ockham*, trans. and ed. Eugene R. Fairweather, Library of Christian Classics (Philadelphia: Westminster Press, 1956), 283.

21. Marshall, *Beyond Retribution*, 44.

22. Tim Gorringe, *God's Just Vengeance: Crime, Violence and the Rhetoric of Salvation* (Cambridge: Cambridge University Press, 1996), 83–219.

23. Emile Durkheim, *The Division of Labor in Society* (New York: Macmillan, 1933), 85–86, 99–100.

24. Walter Wink, *Engaging the Powers: Discernment and Resistance in a World of Domination* (Minneapolis: Fortress Press, 1992), 13–31.

25. For further exploration of this theme, see Thomas Porter, ed. *Conflict and Communion: Reconciliation and Restorative Justice at Christ's Table* (Nashville: Discipleship Resources, 2006) and Thomas Porter, *The Spirit and Art of Conflict Transformation, Creating a Culture of JustPeace* (Nashville: Upper Room Books, 2010).

III
RITUALS OF RECONCILIATION

6

RITUAL AND RECONCILIATION

Kate Dooley, OP

The sacrament of reconciliation was the last of the sacramental rites to be revised after the Second Vatican Council and was promulgated on the First Sunday of Advent, December 2, 1973. The introduction to the rite provides a theology of the sacrament of reconciliation that reflects a broad understanding of the nature and purpose of the sacrament. The theology places the emphasis on God's action and God's unconditional love for us that calls for a response, for a continuous ongoing conversion, a transformation of heart and of life. Catechesis, at the time of promulgation, generally focused on the three forms of celebration of the sacrament rather than the theology of the rite. For Catholics of all ages, who were used to "going to confession," the option of three different forms offered in the rite, particularly the communal form, was definitely an innovation.

The introduction to the rite also presents a much broader understanding of the meaning of the word and practice of "confession" by returning to the early church in which confession was, not only admission of sins committed against God and one another, but was an affirmation of faith in a merciful and loving God. To name the sacrament, "reconciliation," is to restore an ancient term found in the New Testament and in the early documents of the church, describing a ministry of Jesus that is now given to the Christian community.

So if anyone is in Christ, there is a new creation: everything old has passed away; see, everything has become new! All this is from God, who reconciled us to himself through Christ, and has given us the ministry of reconciliation; that is, in Christ God was reconciling the world to himself, not counting their trespasses against them, and entrusting the message of reconciliation to us (2 Cor 5:17–19).

What is this "ministry of reconciliation?" Vatican II, in the *Constitution on the Liturgy*, said very little about the sacrament of reconciliation, only that the sacrament was to be revised in order that it might more clearly express both the nature and effect of the sacrament.[1] By 1974, the theologians responsible for the revision of the *Rite of Penance* had studied the history and practice of the sacrament and offered a rite that had three distinct ritual forms. The first was individual confession that may include the reading of scripture in order that the penitent may be "called to conversion and to confidence in God's mercy" (RP, 15–21). A second form of the rite includes individual confession within the context of a communal celebration, and a third form is a communal celebration with general absolution. But more than additional forms, the introduction to the *Rite* points out that the heart of reconciliation is conversion by which one "begins to consider, judge, and arrange one's life according to the holiness and love of God made manifest in Jesus" (RP, 6a).

The mystery of reconciliation is expressed in many ways in the life of the Church and is fostered primarily in the three sacraments of reconciliation that have a particular focus on conversion of life: baptism, penance, and Eucharist. Baptism incorporates us into the life of God and makes us members of the community. The sacrament of penance is a serious striving to perfect the grace of baptism so that we may be ever more faithful followers of Jesus Christ. Penance, for those in grave sin, restores this baptismal grace. In the early centuries of the church, penance culminated in "reconciliation to the altar." Participation in the Eucharist, therefore, was the tangible expression of the reconciliation of the sinner. Contemporary theology restores the perspective that the Eucharist affirms and celebrates reconciliation and is a means of continuing conversion. These perspectives are addressed in the revision of the *Rite of Penance*, particularly in the emphasis on God's mercy and love in the theology of the rite, found in the introduction and evident in the prayers of the ritual.

The *Rite* also places a strong emphasis on the supernatural bond that brings about the solidarity of the community, both in sin and in holiness. The ecclesial emphasis of the rite underlines the need for dependence on one another.

> Penance always entails reconciliation with our brothers and sisters who are always harmed by our sins...and since they "frequently join together to commit injustice it is only fitting that they should help each other in doing penance so that freed from sin by the grace of Christ they may work with all people of good will for justice and peace in the world. (RP, 5)

Despite a renewed theology of reconciliation and a revised ritual, various surveys in the 1970s and 1980s indicated that participation in the sacrament was problematic. Authors writing on the sacrament in the United States began to quickly speak of a "crisis" in the sacrament. As James O'Toole notes, "Perhaps the most striking feature of the history of confession in the United States is the speed with which it collapsed. Almost overnight, a sacrament that had been at the center of American Catholic practice became rare."[2] Perhaps another "striking feature" is that over fifty years later, the church in the United States is perhaps still at the same impasse.

In 1988, the United States Bishops' Conference, in an effort to face the issue of the crisis of reconciliation, sent questionnaires to all U.S. Bishops, to a random sample of twenty-five hundred priests nationwide, and to a segment of the laity in three dioceses.³ Although this survey is almost twenty-five years old, the responses sound contemporary. In general, the bishops who responded indicated that the decline in participation in the sacrament of reconciliation was generally due to confusion over the nature of sin and uncertainty about what is morally right or wrong. Disagreement with certain of the Church's moral teachings on particular issues also contributed to the lack of participation. Liturgical and pastoral changes and the experience of reconciliation by other means were not seen, at that time, as significant factors affecting the reception of the sacrament.

The priests who responded to the bishops' survey indicated that there was, in the past, "an excessive sense of guilt associated with the sacrament." Other responses from priests indicated that confessions often seemed somewhat superficial and unreflective of the penitent's actual life. In reality, the confessions were a carryover of the rote confessions made as children. One woman's response to the survey was indicative of this viewpoint. She acknowledged that the sacrament became meaningless to her when she began to realize that she was still confessing the same sins that she had confessed as a child, except that she no longer said, "I disobeyed my mother!"

Many priests generally appreciated the personal dimension of the sacrament in Rite One because it provided an opportunity for spiritual direction and dialogue with the penitent. Other priest respondents reported that they did not feel they had adequate training to provide the kind of response that was sometimes needed in speaking with the penitent. Other respondents noted that people today experience reconciliation in a variety of other ways, particularly in the celebration of the Eucharist. Although the Eucharist is not ordered to the forgiveness of mortal sins, many people realized that the "Eucharist cannot unite us to Christ without at the same time cleansing us from past sins and preserving us from future sins."⁴ Moreover, "daily conversion and penance find their source and nourishment in the Eucharist, for in it is made present the sacrifice of Christ which has reconciled us with God. Through the Eucharist those who live from the life of Christ are fed and strengthened."[5]

The survey also noted that there had been few diocesan-level initiatives with regard to the sacrament of reconciliation. Most catechesis of adults has occurred through their involvement in the preparation of their children for the sacrament of reconciliation. Some dioceses had programs of outreach to alienated Catholics that included sessions on the sacrament of reconciliation and led some individuals to return to the sacrament. Moreover, there had been few pastoral letters from the bishops on the sacrament of reconciliation. Workshops for the clergy on the sacrament were last held in many dioceses when the *Ordo Paenitentiae* was introduced in 1974. Many bishops recognized that the demands placed upon the priests in the proper and full celebration of the rite of individual confession are significant, and many priests have not received training in those skills which would serve them well in this ministry.[6] At the time of the *Rite of Penance*'s publication, the focus was placed on "the how to" of celebrating the three forms. Very little attention appeared to be given to the theology of the rite found in the introduction. The new practice, therefore, was often undermined by an old theology.

Pope John Paul II, in his apostolic letter, *Novo Millenio Ineunte*, written in 2000, called for "renewed pastoral courage for the rediscovery of the compassionate heart of Christ." In the letter, the pope stated:

> My invitation then was to make every effort to face the crisis of the "sense of sin" apparent in today's culture. But I was even more insistent in calling for a rediscovery of Christ as *mysterium pietatis*, the one in whom God shows us his compassionate heart and reconciles us fully with himself. It is this face of Christ that must be rediscovered through the Sacrament of Penance, which for the faithful is "the ordinary way of obtaining for-

giveness and the remission of serious sins committed after Baptism."[7] (No. 37)

Assessment of the attitudes of the laity with regard to the rite of individual confession was undertaken by The Center for Applied Research in 2008. The study, titled *Sacraments Today: Belief and Practice among U.S. Catholics,*[8] indicated that three quarters of the Catholics in the United States report that they never participate in the sacrament of reconciliation or that they do so less than once a year. This study and several others on the sacrament again offer a wide variety of reasons for the situation: a changed understanding of sin or a loss of a sense of sin—at the very least, confusion about what is sinful; disagreement with the teachings of the Church on a number of issues; individualism in our society; the experience of reconciliation in other ways, past difficulty with a confessor, inconvenient times for the celebration of the sacrament, and the list continues.

Some of these concerns are addressed in the revision of the *Rite of Penance,* particularly in the emphasis on God's mercy and love in the theology of the rite, found in the introduction and manifest in the prayers of the ritual. The *Rite* also places an emphasis on the supernatural bond, which brings about solidarity of the community in sin and in holiness. Pope John Paul's call for the rediscovery of "the compassionate heart of Christ" is a reminder that in the sacrament of reconciliation, the faithful "obtain from the mercy of God pardon for their sins, and at the same time are reconciled with the church whom they wounded by their sins and who works for their conversion by charity, example and prayer" (RP, 4). The introduction to the *Rite* proposes that there is a need to go beyond an understanding of the sacrament of reconciliation as comprised of only the penitent's confession of sinfulness and the reception of absolution. The sacrament is worship. The focus needs to be placed on God's action, which is manifested in God's infinite love.

The sacramental moment, moreover, does not end with the

words of absolution. In order for the sacrament of healing "to truly achieve its purpose among Christ's faithful, it must take root in their whole lives and move them to more fervent service of God and neighbor" (RP, 7b). The sacrament is not only about the forgiveness of sin; it is about conversion of life. The ritual makes "sacramentally present Jesus' call to conversion, the first step in returning to the Father from whom one has strayed by sin."[9] The imperative of the Gospel, "Repent and believe the good news" is a call to deepening faith, to a life in Jesus Christ that is begun in baptism, strengthened and celebrated in the Eucharist, and lived out each day in "service of God and neighbor." The ultimate purpose of the sacrament is that "Those who are freed from sin by the grace of Christ may work with all people of good will for peace and justice" (RP, 5).

The penance imposed in the *Rite of Penance* is to be a means of ongoing conversion. In assigning a penance to the individual, the *Rite* indicates that this act of penance corresponds to the needs of each individual because it serves, not only to make up for the past, but also as a help to ongoing conversion. Often, the penance given is the recitation of prayers, but the *Rite* also suggests other forms such as "service of one's neighbor and works of mercy that would underline the fact that sin and its forgiveness have a social aspect" (RP, 18). The focus of the sacrament is, not only the forgiveness of sin, but also is to be an important means of conversion of heart and life.

One woman at a recent parish meeting spoke about the experience of being given a penance that included an action as well as prayer. The confessor recommended, as a penance, that she volunteer once or twice a week for the next month in a soup kitchen in one of the neighboring parishes that daily provided food for the homeless. With some hesitation, she went to the kitchen. Now, three years later, she not only continues to serve once or twice each week but has joined the parish because she has found it truly to be a "means to conversion of heart and life."

Catechesis, today, needs to be based on the theology of the *Rite of Penance*, which places the focus on God's action in the ritual of reconciliation. The scriptures, read with the penitent in each of the forms of the *Rite*, present profound scriptural images of who God is for us. The Good Shepherd, the forgiving Father, Jesus' forgiveness of the sinful woman, the parable of the lost coin, Zaccheus the tax collector, the woman in adultery, and many other images manifest the gratuitous love of God for us. Perhaps the issue is that many people may not really believe that they are loved by God. Perhaps some adults are like the child, who upon hearing the story of the prodigal son and the forgiving father, said he thought it was a trick. His view was that "when they got back into the house that kid would really get it!" Most of the other children thought it was a big relief. They "bet the son sure didn't expect a welcome like that!" Perhaps in the world in which we live, it is difficult to believe in an unconditional love. One aspect of catechesis is to help, not only children, but also adults to believe in God's unconditional love for them, which is made evident in all the scriptural images used in the *Rite* that underline God's mercy and love as the purpose of the sacrament of reconciliation.

> In the sacrament of Penance the Father receives the repentant son who comes back to him, Christ places the lost sheep on his shoulder and brings it back to the sheepfold, and the Holy Spirit sanctifies this temple of God again or lives more fully within it. This is finally expressed in a renewed and more fervent sharing of the Lord's Table, and there is great joy at the banquet of God's church over the son who has returned from afar. (RP, 6d)

The sacrament does not end with the words of absolution. In order for the sacrament of healing "to truly achieve its purpose among Christ's faithful, it must take root in their whole lives and move them to more fervent service of God and neighbor" (RP, 7b). The sacrament is not only about the forgiveness of sin; it is about conversion of life. The ritual makes sacramentally present Jesus' call to conversion.[10] The imperative of the gospel, "...repent, and believe in the good news" (Mark 1:15), is a call to deepening faith, to a life in Jesus Christ that is begun in baptism, strengthened and celebrated in the Eucharist, and lived out each day in "service of God and neighbor." The ultimate purpose of the sacrament is that "Those who are freed from sin by the grace of Christ may work with all people of good will for peace and justice" (RP, 5).

What is the future? In *Saying Amen: A Mystagogy of Sacrament,* Sister Kathleen Hughes states: "Perhaps the most serious lesson to be learned from these last several decades is the almost total lack of thoughtful and sustained catechesis on the liturgy."[11] This statement challenges all catechists and pastoral ministers to begin to give serious study to the rite of reconciliation so that through this sacrament, the Christian community might come to a deeper realization of God's love that will enable them to "work with all people of good will for peace and justice."

Notes

1. Constitution on the Sacred Liturgy, no. 72.

2. James O'Toole, ed., *Habits of Devotion: Catholic Religious Practice in Twentieth Century* (Ithaca, NY: Cornell University Press, 2004).

3. United States Catholic Conference of Bishops Pastoral Research and Practices Committee, *Origins* 19: no. 38 (February 22, 1990), 614–26.

4. *Catechism of the Catholic Church,* no.1395.

5. Ibid., no. 1436.

6. James O'Toole, "The Court of Conscience: American Catholics and Confession, 1900–1975," in *Habits of Devotion: Catholic Religious Practice in Twentieth Century* (Ithaca, NY: Cornell University Press, 2004), 174.

7. *Reconciliatio et paenitentia,* Post-Synodal Exhortation (December 3, 1984), no. 28.

8. Center for Applied Research in the Apostolate, *Sacraments Today: Belief and Practice among U.S. Catholics* (Washington, D.C.: Georgetown University, 2005).

9. *Catechism*, no. 1423.

10. Ibid.

11. Kathleen Hughes, RSCJ, *Saying Amen: A Mystagogy of Sacrament* (Chicago: Liturgy Training Publications, 1999), xviii.

7

EXPANDING THE RITES OF RECONCILIATION

Peter E. Fink, SJ

When the *Rite of Penance* (*Ordo Paenitentiae*) was revised in 1975, it clearly expanded our understanding of this sacrament. Following the mandate of the Vatican II *Constitution on the Sacred Liturgy* (SC, 72), the *Rite of Penance* aimed to present rituals that "more clearly express the nature and effects of this sacrament." In the *Rite of Penance*, what is offered are distinct ritual forms that together seek to effect a gospel response to human sinfulness.

In addition to these sacramental forms, the *Rite of Penance* includes several Penitential Services, such as, for children, for the sick, for Advent, and for Lent. And it removed from ordinary celebrations of the sacrament, responses that belong to particular moments, such as absolution from censure and dispensation for irregularities.

Structure of the Rite of Penance

The first ritual form, as most people are aware, is the *Reconciliation of Individual Penitents*. This places the celebration of the sacrament firmly under the Word of God, and reminds us that both priest and penitent together must listen to the Word before anything else is enacted. It was that Word, as Paul notes, that accomplished forgiveness and reconciliation (2 Cor 5:18). The second ritual form is the *Reconciliation of Several Penitents*. This is designed "to empathize the relation of the sacrament to the community" (Decree). And the third ritual form is the *Reconciliation of Several Penitents with General Confession and Absolution*. This is to be used on special occasions.

For a brief while after its promulgation, all three rites were employed in the Church. The first form gradually brought people to shift from the legal model, which had dominated the preconciliar practice of confession, to this liturgical model, which placed the gospel Word as primary. To skip the second form for a minute, the third form began to be used for two reasons: to reconcile large numbers who had been separated from the church and to provide the sacrament when there were simply not enough priests available. The second form developed in two different directions. If it was to hold the community together until the end of the service, the presentation of sinfulness had to be limited and the interchange with the confessor restricted, which made it closer to the third form. If it was to allow the individual confessions to unfold as needed, the last part of the service would have to be done on another occasion. And this made it closer to the first form. On the one hand, therefore, the second form was the most promising and yet, on the other hand, it was the most problematic.

Two Theologies of Reconciliation

In the introduction to the *Rite*, two different theologies are in evidence. The first is a theology of remembrance, following the Jewish and Christian prayer of memory and hope. "The celebration of this sacrament is thus always an act in which the Church proclaims its faith, gives thanks to God for the freedom with which Christ has made us free, and offers its life as a spiritual sacrifice in praise of God's glory, as it hastens to meet the Lord Jesus" (RP Intro, 8). The second deals with conversion and new beginnings. "The follower of Christ who has sinned...should above all be converted to God with his whole heart. This inner conversion of the heart embraces sorrow for sin and the intent to lead a new life. It is expressed in confession made to (a minister of) the Church, due satisfaction and amendment of life" (Intro, 6).

If we listen to each theology, a different mode of procedure will be needed as we engage the three ritual forms. In a theology of remembrance, the mode of interaction is not unlike the Eucharist itself. What is important is that we remember that, in Christ, all sin is forgiven. This requires a proclamation of the Word such as 2 Corinthians 5, which reminds us that as forgiven sinners, we are called to be heralds of reconciliation. Our own presentation of sinfulness need not be elaborate. The reconciliation that Christ has accomplished is more crucial to proclaim. Now following this theology, an experience of the sacrament in common would be held as the primary celebration event, where people who had experienced the sacrament on a more individual level would come to witness to the community that Christ's healing and forgiveness does indeed happen.

On the other hand, in a theology of conversion and new beginnings, what would dominate is the individual need to express one's sinfulness before God and to follow a pattern more like spiritual direction to allow that healing work to slowly unfold in one's life. This would require scriptures, such as the healing of the blind man or the cure of the crippled man, and all of the things that belong to individual forgiveness: confession, amendment of life, satisfaction, and finally, thanksgiving. Following this theology, the first form would be the most proper. And it probably should not be seen as a single ritual event, but as a process. It might need several enactments of the sacrament to move toward forgiveness and reconciliation.

As I have said, when the *Rite of Penance* was revised in 1975, it clearly expanded our understanding of this sacrament. These three rituals do expand our understanding somewhat if, indeed, the rituals themselves are freely used. The question I am raising in this essay is just how imaginative we have been in receiving the promise of the *Rite of Penance*. Have we explored all the possibilities for forgiveness and reconciliation that are possible?

A Vatican II Reminder

There is another citation from the *Constitution on the Sacred Liturgy* that influences my concern. When speaking about the communal nature of the liturgy, it says: "It must be emphasized that rites which are meant to be celebrated in common, with the faithful present and actively participating, should as far as possible be celebrated in that way rather than by an individual and quasi-privately. This applies with special force to the celebration of Mass (even though every Mass has of itself a public and social nature) and to the administration of the sacraments" (SC, 26). This stands in contrast to a statement later on in the introduction to the *Rite of Penance*, which has become the primary discipline of the Church: "An individual, complete confession and the receiving of absolution remain the only ordinary way for the faithful to obtain reconciliation with God and the Church, unless physical or moral impossibility excuses from this kind of confession" (Intro, 31).

I fear that this discipline of the Church keeps us from imagining a larger view of this sacrament, both in terms of the rituals in the *Rite of Penance* that are actually given, and beyond those rituals toward even more ways in which the gospel can confront human sinfulness. It is essential that we get beyond that current discipline.

Exploring the Fullness of the Sacrament of Forgiveness

Let me return to a text from Paul that I cited earlier. This text is equally important in the establishment of the *Rite of Penance* as is the more familiar texts on the giving of the keys. This text clearly gives us a mandate for a rich collection of sacramental rituals, much more than are given in the current *Rite of Penance*. Paul cites:

All this is from God, who reconciled us to himself through Christ, and has given us the ministry of reconciliation; that is, in Christ God was reconciling the world to himself, not counting their trespasses against them, and entrusting the message of reconciliation to us. So we are ambassadors for Christ, since God is making his appeal through us; we entreat you on behalf of Christ, be reconciled to God. (2 Cor 5:18–20)

This text establishes the fundamental principle of my concern with the sacrament of reconciliation and forgiveness. Through Christ, God does not hold sin against us. In Christ, all sin is forgiven. It also establishes a primary mandate for all believers. First, to take that statement seriously—that God has, in Christ, already reconciled us to himself—and second, that we must, therefore, become ourselves ministers of reconciliation.

This tells me that the sacrament of forgiveness and reconciliation has two principal purposes. The first, it must alter our own self-imagination to know that things for which we might be truly sorry, and rightly so, are set before a God who has already forgiven them. "Who reconciled us to himself through Christ." If you do not come from the celebration—however the celebration is enacted—without hearing that statement of our faith within you, the celebration has not yet succeeded. Second—again however the sacrament is enacted—it needs to take us beyond ourselves and our need to a forgotten part of the Lord's Prayer—as we forgive those who sin against us. Paul puts it: "we are ambassadors for Christ, since God is making his appeal through us" (2 Cor 5:20).

On Seeking Forgiveness

When Jesus was asked to give the greatest commandments in the law, he said: "'Love the Lord your God with all your heart, and with all your soul, and with all your mind.' This is the greatest and first commandment. And the second is like it: 'You shall love your neighbor as yourself.' On these two commandments hang all the law and the prophets" (Matt 22:37–40). There are three loves here

97

that need to grow together. You cannot love God and hate your neighbor; you cannot love your neighbor and hate yourself.

I would like to say the same about forgiveness. According to our own religious faith, we know that God is merciful and forgives us all. Effectively announcing that is what the gospel is about. Effectively announcing that is what the sacrament of penance (whether called confession, forgiveness, or reconciliation) is about. The journey of forgiveness rests more on us. Like the mandate to love God, our neighbor, and ourselves, there is a similar mandate to forgive God, forgive our neighbor, and forgive ourselves. All three need to grow together.

This is something I learned years ago from Dorothy Sayers, I think from the *Mind of the Maker*, though I have never again found the actual source. It was about forgiving God, forgiving our neighbor, and forgiving ourselves. Forgiving God, because God does not always do what we expect God to do. Forgiving our neighbor, because they do not do what we expect them to do. Forgiving ourselves, because we do not do what we expect ourselves to do. The phrase I remember most: "To know that is forgiveness."

Now, all this is wonderful on a theoretical level. But the question that it leads to is this: When people participate in the sacrament of penance, what do they experience today? Knowing that the levels of experience are many, let me offer a few levels that come to mind.

I think of people who present things routinely, sometimes with qualms of conscience but most of the time not. Therefore, they experience the sacrament routinely, as a check on their progress and sometimes as a guide forward. It is like spiritual direction, though with a focus more on the negative and its repair. For them, a personal approach is most appropriate.

I think of others who have a serious reality that they need to present, which could be of recent vintage or from a long time ago. Things like: "last week, after having too much to drink, I hit my wife." Or, "thirty years ago, I realized I was homosexual, and since the Church says it is wrong, I left the church. But now something is drawing me back." Such situations are for more than a checkup. They really call for what the instruction calls "new beginnings." What they are looking for will take much longer than a single celebration of the sacrament.

In either case, and in many more like it, the sacrament seems to be limited to one's personal sin, and how the person might come to experience forgiveness in the sacrament. That is one important promise of the sacrament. Yet there are so many other realities that people sense as sin, such as social sin, antagonisms among groups, even what I have frequently called "sin too large." Yet while they may enter into the moral consciousness that people have, they are not particularly represented in the current patterns of the *Rite of Penance*. They, too, need the gospel to be spoken upon them so that healing might occur.

On Understanding Sin

So a first step in expanding the rites of sacramental forgiveness must be a journey to understand sin in our day and the way it touches the human heart. We must remember that, however the sacrament is celebrated, it is always a responsive sacrament. No one takes medicine for an illness they do not have. No one should engage in the sacrament of forgiveness for the sins they do not have. The required form should fit the required need.

Too often, people regard themselves as sinners because they have done things that are on a list somewhere that says they are sins. Those lists can be an important part of the journey, but that is a first step, not a final response. Ultimately, you understand your sin when you focus in on the love of Christ. Sin turns you away from Christ. Reconciliation turns you back to Christ.

Years ago, my moral theology professor looked at the act of masturbation to explore how wide the possibilities of experience might be. He was able to see it, not as a univocal act that is always and everywhere to be understood as seriously sinful. Rather he saw it as having several possible understandings: (a) as a turning in on oneself, (b) as an act of disobedience, (c) as a biological act that had no moral significance, (d) even as an act of love. That kind of sophistication, most people do not have. That kind of sophistication people need to have if they will appreciate the forgiveness and the promise of this sacrament.

The Psychology of Forgiveness

A second step is to understand the psychology of forgiveness. What has to happen for you to forgive? There is a superficial way to understand forgiveness, and a more profound way. The superficial way is to minimize the offense as in, "I guess it was not that important." In many cases, the best way toward forgiveness here is to see the offense in terms of things that are much more important and much more serious. A more profound way is to look at the offense in all its seriousness, to recognize the anger that the offense can bring about. There, the task is to find a way beyond the offense and the anger into the freedom that will not allow yourself to get stuck within the offense and anger.

The first is a form of practical forgiveness. It locates the offense in terms of a larger world. Most forms of forgiveness are simply that. The second is more difficult to achieve. When the offense is such that it cannot be made small, what is required is a way of imagining that allows the offense to be serious and yet allows oneself to go forward with life.

Just one example of the first: a friend did not show up at an important event, and had no excuse. As much as that can hurt, recalling the level of friendship allows a forgiveness of that event and precisely preserves the friendship.

An example of the second: a person is victimized by a rape, which could bring her into a world of anger, suspicion, and fear of relationships. You can never minimize the effect of that rape. What forgiveness might help you to do is to find freedom beyond the rape to enter relationships again. This second example will require lots of time to happen.

Paths to Forgiveness

We need to find paths to forgiveness from the personal journey through one's inner turmoil to the communal experience of remembrance and hope. This needs, first of all, a deep sense that, in Christ, all sin is forgiven. We need to recognize that the primary aim of the sacrament is always to hear that element of faith effectively. And finally, we need to recognize that any path that helps us hear that word effectively shares in the sacramental tradition of forgiveness (confession, reconciliation, etc.). It can never be limited to the discipline that is currently active in the Church.

We have seen that in the *Rite of Penance*, three rituals are given to celebrate the sacrament. We have also noted the current discipline of the Church that the only true and proper form for the sacrament is the private form. This leaves the celebration of the sacrament in its minimal form. And unfortunately, the practice of this sacrament is also at its minimum. But the need for forgiveness and reconciliation remains quite strong. It just does not have the proper vehicles to address that need.

Expanding the Ways of Forgiveness

So let's explore a bit. I must confess, however, that this exploration is nothing new. It is not like doing research for a work that will soon be published. It is, in part, at least a resurrection of a word already published, though little came from that first publication. Years ago, several of us explored ways of expanding all sacramental rituals; I edited two, one on sacramental anointing and one on reconciliation.[1] Much that is presented here is a revival of that sacramental venture.

The first possible expansion grew out of the current form two. As I mentioned above, at least two possibilities suggest themselves. If it was to hold the community together until the end of the service, the presentation of sinfulness had to be limited and

101

the interchange with the confessor restricted. This offended those who felt a full presentation of sinfulness was required, but it did allow a liturgical service to come to its proper conclusion. On the other hand, if the service were to allow the individual confessions to unfold as needed, the last part of the service would be best done on another occasion. This offended the liturgical purists, but it showed that no sacrament achieves its effect instantaneously. It could unfold over several days or even weeks.

A modification on rite two would explore a communal service that brought together several priests who would hear the confessions. Only the pastor or principle presider would be set apart from the crowd. The people, after their confession to individual priests, would then go to the pastor or presider for the laying on of hands. This combination, and a final prayer of thanksgiving, paralleled the baptismal rite, where the confession and absolution would be analogous to the bathing and the post-baptismal anointing, and the laying on of hands and prayer analogous to confirmation.

An ever greater variant, made important where the availability of priests has become so limited, would be to train lay men and women to hear the confession and to offer words of encouragement and support. Then both the confessor and the penitent would go together to the pastor for absolution and a laying on of hands. A prayer of presentation by the confessor and a statement of sorrow and repentance by the penitent would warrant the pastor's absolution.

Another mode of exploration brings us to a hospital situation, where—so frequently—lay women and men provide the reading of scripture, offer words of encouragement and support, and distribute the food of Eucharist. This is already the beginnings of the sacrament, not just something that prepares for the sacrament. But at some point in that ongoing ministry, the person might feel the need for the larger Church to be represented as well. A priest might then be called, but his response must always include the work of the regular chaplain as well as what the priest will now bring. It is important that the priest complements the work of a lay hospital chaplain, and that the two are seen together as sacramental ministers.

Yet another exploration seeks to address what I often call "sin too large." It could be the atrocities of war, such as, the holocaust or suicidal bombings of civilians. It could be global exploitation that leaves children starving and parents in a stage of hopelessness. "Sin too large" is easy to pin down, but it is hard to figure out who is responsible. Yet it is sin nonetheless, and it, too, needs to be addressed by the healing power of Christ.

What I suggested is a liturgy of Christian Atonement, styled on the Jewish Day of Atonement, where "sin too large" is humbly placed into the mercy of our God. A good place to enact it would be during the feast of Christ the King. I suggested that water be used as the primary symbol of reconciliation, coupled of course by the people who engage the water. Step one was for our own personal part in the enactment of "sin too large"; come forth and wash your hands. Step two was for the actions of the church, who either themselves were involved or who failed to do in relation to "sin too large." For this, the altar would be washed in atonement. Finally, step three, the world's involvement in "sin too large"; sprinkle the four corners of the earth in humble prayer.

This could include a service at home as well, perhaps styled on the Jewish Seder meal. Christians tend to be remiss when it comes to prayer at our meals—a quick blessing if at all. Yet the meal itself is or should be a time of reconciliation. Why not expand its scope to grievances beyond this immediate gathering? Why not expand its scope to "sin too large?"

Another kind of need for reconciliation has to do with the reconciliation of groups. This is particularly useful in ecumenical settings, where there are so many differences that keep us apart. Reconciliation here requires a different kind of ritual interaction. Some kind of ritual might start the process, but it will be more a ritual of open-mindedness and hope than a ritual of healing and gratitude. Throughout the process of mutual interaction, other rituals may be enacted, which might note some accomplishment, but which will be more encouragement than anything else. Only at the end, when some kind of reconciliation is achieved, can a ritual of thanksgiving be enacted. But the movement, nonetheless, is a constant movement of healing.

Another suggestion was made to capture the season of Lent as an ongoing ritual of forgiveness and reconciliation. The day of ashes, Ash Wednesday, sets the stage for the possibility of confession, which would take place throughout the season. It could take place in connection with the scrutinies, which are the first enactment of reconciliation for those entering the Church. But this would not yet be the complete sacramental journey. The full reconciliation would take place on Holy Thursday, restoring a classic time of reconciliation in the West, enacting, of course, the biblical stance to seek reconciliation before bringing one's gifts to the altar.

Still another suggestion was for a festival of forgiveness and reconciliation, following the tradition of a mission or a novena. Scripture, homily, and ritual movement would be the structures of prayer during this time of retreat. Interspersed, however, would be conversation and contemplation: conversation to explore with fellow journey-folks the various needs for reconciliation among them; and contemplation, allowing God to enter the heart of each with the peace that only Christ can give.

There are many other experiences that call for forgiveness and reconciliation, asking only that the gospel seek ways to address them: couples with disputes in their marriage, families who must deal with issues of discipline with their children, people who are afraid, people who are lost, people who are confused, people who are alienated. If we remember that, in Christ, all sin is already forgiven, then we have no choice but to find ways to effectively express that forgiveness to others. Remember, reconciliation is the mission of the church.

Can History Help in the Quest?

It is a good question whether a history of the sacrament would be helpful in mapping out ways to respond, since the usual presentation of history is in its narrowest sacramental sense. That does not offer much by way of exploration. But most recently, I came upon a fresh view of the history that can suggest some ways of expanding this sacramental reach. Annemarie Kidder, in her *Making Confession, Hearing Confession: A History of the Cure of Souls*,[2] does present some interesting possibilities. She offers, of course, a standard view of the sacrament. But she also presents other modes of opening up the Church's gospel response to sin in ways larger than the traditional look at the sacrament.

She explores, for example, the full range of spiritual direction. In the Celtic world, for example, where lay women and men as well as monks guided prayer and penance, and offered words of wisdom. Or in the world of the sixteenth century reform, where she looks at confession, preaching, and other ways in which ordinary Christians admonished each other. Or her presentation of Ignatius of Loyola and the tradition of the Spiritual Exercises, with their invitation to conversion, healing, and apostolic mission.

I said in a review of this work, that Kidder does more than treat sacramental confession. She highlights the women and men throughout the history of the Church who served as confessor, guide, source of prayer, wisdom, and healing. Her work will surely serve this kind of exploration.

Conclusion

At the end, let me simply pose some questions to keep the conversation going. We constantly need to ask in our hearts, what is it like to feel the need for forgiveness? Not just to know about it in our mind, but to feel what it is to cry out for healing. And we need to ask, whose forgiveness do you need? Certainly the forgiveness of God for those who feel alienated from God. Certainly the forgiveness of the neighbor, where my own sinfulness might have affected them. Certainly, perhaps most difficult of all, forgiveness of self. I do not have much forgiveness to offer to either God or to my neighbor if I cannot forgive myself.

Some further questions are: How would you like to pursue that forgiveness? What do you expect to feel when you have experienced forgiveness? What rituals might arise in our midst as ways to enact the forgiveness that is needed? The sacrament is always a responsive sacrament. It always responds to the need of forgiveness if and when that need is presented.

At any rate, these are some of the things we need to do if we would explore or expand the rites of reconciliation. The purpose is always very simple: to allow the gospel of Jesus Christ to touch any and all sinfulness, however people experience it and however they seek a word that heals.

Notes

1. *Alternative Futures for Worship*, vol. 4, *Reconciliation*, ed. Peter E. Fink, SJ (Collegeville, MN: Liturgical Press, 1987).

2. (Collegeville, MN: Liturgical Press [Glazier], 2010).

IV

ECUMENICAL AND INTERFAITH PERSPECTIVES

8

RECONCILIATION AMONG THE CHURCHES
Where We Need to Go and What We'll Need for the Journey

Thomas P. Ryan, CSP

In the New Testament, the word "reconciliation" is used to describe the changed relations between God and humanity that are the result of the death and resurrection of Jesus Christ. The source of reconciliation is the God of love, and the sphere in which reconciliation is an experienced reality is the new divine community—the Church—being built up by the activity of the Spirit of God.[1]

In Greek, reconciliation is the term normally used for the resumption of common life by husband and wife, and its daring application to the relationship between God and us is uniquely biblical, underlining its peculiarly personal and intimate quality.[2]

In other words, the Church is the community of those who, because of Christ, are no longer separated. It is a contradiction in terms to speak of "separated Christians." Reconciliation and unity are of the very nature of the Church of Christ. To be "in communion of life" with one another as Christians is our vocation. Our communion with each other is linked with an infinitely deeper one from which it is inseparable: our communion with the Father and the Son in the Holy Spirit. What this means is common participation in the same benefits, shared possession of

109

the same treasure. Though our churches stand in proximity to one another, we remain largely strangers to each other. We have not yet grasped the meaning—resumption of common life—of the kind of sharing implied by the word "reconciliation."

For the last thirty-one years, I have served as an ambassador of reconciliation to Christians in Canada and the U.S.: fifteen years at the Canadian Centre for Ecumenism; five at Unitas, an Ecumenical Centre for Spirituality co-founded by eight denominations (also located in Montreal); and since 2000, at the Paulist North American Office for Ecumenical and Interfaith Relations in Washington, DC. During this time, the work for reconciliation among Christians has gone through various seasons.

At the World Council of Churches' (WCC) last General Assembly in Porto Allegre, Brazil in 2006, the Moderator of the WCC Central Committee, His Holiness Aram I, catholicos of the See of Cilicia of the Armenian Apostolic Church, painted with broad brushstrokes a picture of the present context in the ecumenical movement. Mainstream Christianity is aging and shrinking. The institutional church is losing much of its impact on society. Divisions in many churches on ethical, social, and pastoral issues are creating confusion and estrangement. The divide between "belonging" and "believing" is growing.[3]

"We have entered a new period of ecumenical history," said Aram. "The ecumenical landscape is undergoing rapid and radical change: traditional ecumenical institutions are losing their motivation and interest; new ecumenical models and norms are emerging; new ecumenical alliances and partnerships are being formed; and new ecumenical agendas are being set. The ecumenical panorama today represents a new picture."[4]

In short, we are on a journey. The panorama Aram refers to is not a still photo but a moving film. As an outdoorsman and canoe camper, working with the journey metaphor comes naturally. The way forward in the movement for Christian unity *is* a wilderness, and we have by no means yet completed the journey. I would like to propose an eight-point strategy for what lies ahead. Most of what you hear may feel like *Back to the Future* because the way forward involves what some at Vatican II called *ressourcement*—a return to the early wellsprings from which the vision of the community called "Church" emerged; a return to the fundamental sources of motivation that gave birth to the modern ecumenical movement.

Look Again at the Map and Re-clarify the Destination

Key reference points on the map are the WCC Constitution, the WCC New Delhi statement, and the Second Vatican Council's Decree on Ecumenism. The first purpose of the World Council of Churches, according to its Constitution, is "to call the churches to the goal of visible unity in one faith and one Eucharistic fellowship expressed in worship and common life in Christ, and to advance toward that unity in order that the world may believe."[5] In his encyclical letter *On Commitment to Ecumenism*, Pope John Paul II is in full agreement: "The ultimate goal of the ecumenical movement is to reestablish full visible unity among all the baptized."[6]

The most often quoted vision statement by the Third WCC General Assembly meeting in New Delhi, India, in 1961, remains a critical reference:

> We believe that the unity which is both God's will and his gift to the Church is being made visible as all in each place who are baptized into Christ Jesus and confess him as Lord and Savior. This unity takes visible form as all are brought by the Holy Spirit into one fully committed fellowship, holding the one apostolic faith, preaching the one gospel, breaking the one bread, joining in common prayer and having a corporate life in reaching out in witness and service to all, and who at the same time are united with the whole Christian fellowship in all places and all ages in such wise that min-

111

istry and members are accepted by all, and that all can
act and speak together as occasion requires for the tasks
to which God calls his people.[7]

The ecumenical vision is concerned with a unity tangible enough
to give witness in the world to God's power to reconcile. It is
driven by a vision of God's people as one people throughout the
earth, abiding in one body, sharing one faith, blessed by common
sacraments, preaching one gospel. At any point along the way, the
instruments that served the Church's unity in one era may lose
their effectiveness, but that does not excuse us from finding new
instruments that will enable us to take the next step along the
way; we must walk in obedience to the gospel—because it is a
question of obedience to the gospel.

The churches' gathered in Porto Allegre for the WCC 2006
General Assembly, reiterated the theme of "full visible unity" in its
important fifteen-paragraph document entitled: "Called to be the
One Church."[8] The concern is that the ecumenical vision is facing a
two-fold crisis: the ecumenical institutions have started to lose con-
tact with the vision, and the vision appears to be vague and
ambiguous. For many, unity is no longer an ecumenical priority,
but rather an academic topic or at best an eschatological goal. The
Council chose to re-emphasize the vital importance of visible unity
by re-embarking on convergence and reception processes.

Start from the Same Place and Speak a Common Language

I would wager that many think the starting point from which
we begin is the need to *create a unity among Christians* where none
presently exists, or to *recreate it* where it has been lost. But such an
understanding—widespread though it may be—is a misconcep-
tion. We need to begin from the same place and use a common
grammar. The place from which we shove off is the ecumenical
conviction that unity belongs to the nature of the Church.

This ecumenical conviction was enunciated by the World Council of Churches' Central Committee meeting in Toronto in 1950, shortly after the founding of the WCC. "The member churches of the World Council believe on the basis of the New Testament that the Church of Christ is one....The churches realize that it is a matter of simple Christian duty for each church to do its utmost for the manifestation of the Church in its oneness, and to work and pray that Christ's purpose for his Church should be fulfilled."[9]

Similarly, in Vatican II's *Dogmatic Constitution on the Church* and *Decree on Ecumenism* (issued on the same day, November 21, 1964, and intended to be interpreted in light of each other), the Catholic Church confesses that, since there is and can be only one Church of Christ, it follows that there can be "churches" only insofar as in some real way they all participate in the reality of the one Church.[10]

Flowing from this ecumenical conviction is a common grammar based upon an *ecumenical indicative and imperative*. The indicative is that, since it is God who assembles the one Church, unity is not something we have to create. It is a present reality given by God to the Church and is presupposed in every effort for unity. The ecumenical imperative is that Christians must give expression to the essential unity of the Church. It must be lived and be made visible.

As a leading contemporary ecumenist, Harding Meyer points out that this dialectic of indicative-imperative is the structure of Pauline thought. "If we live by the Spirit" (which we do), "let us also be guided by the Spirit" (Gal 5:25). If we are one in Christ (which we are), let us also live and act as reconciled people.[11] What makes modern ecumenism different from church unity projected in previous centuries of the second millennium is that it *begins with the ecumenical indicative: the present fact of our unity in Christ.*

The work still before us is a *consequence* of our fundamental communion in Christ, not a *prerequisite* for it. In other words, it is the recognition of how God has bound us in one body that provides the proper setting for the work we undertake through the ecumenical movement.[12] The goal is to allow the unity that

113

already exists among us as God's gift, to become more fully manifest in the way we Christians relate to one another, articulate our faith, worship, and act in the world.

The way into the future for us is to capitalize on every opportunity to live, work, and pray as a reconciled fellowship, whether or not we perceive any practical benefits from it. The future direction is *to live* consistent with who we *are* in every way possible. Unless we recognize that our oneness in Christ is itself a central truth of the gospel, we will not find the stamina to stay engaged for the long haul.

Agree on the Best Kind of Boat for the Journey: A Common Understanding of the Church

We start with a surprising discovery: all the dialogues of the past forty-five years, though held between many partners and without any preconceived plan, are converging on a common concept for understanding the Church: the concept of communion (in Greek, *koinonia*; in Latin, *communio*). All the dialogues define the visible unity of all Christians as *koinonia/communio* in analogy with the Trinity, that is, not as uniformity, but as unity in diversity.[13] Another indicator of the convergence taking place is that the 1985 Synod of Catholic Bishops described communion-ecclesiology as "the central and basic idea of the (Vatican II) Council documents."[14]

In an important statement, entitled "The Unity of the Church as Koinonia: Gift and Calling," the WCC Canberra Assembly (1991) stood fast by the New Delhi vision:

> The unity of the church to which we are called is a koinonia given and expressed in the common confession of the apostolic faith; a common sacramental life entered by the one baptism and celebrated together in one Eucharistic fellowship; a common life in which our

members and ministries are mutually recognized and
reconciled; and a common mission witnessing to the
gospel of God's grace to all people and serving the whole
of creation. The goal of the search for full communion is
realized when all the churches are able to recognize in
one another the one, holy, catholic and apostolic church
in its fullness. This full communion will be expressed on
the local and universal levels through conciliar forms of
life and action. In such communion churches are bound
in all aspects of their life together at all levels in confessing the one faith and engaging in worship and witness,
deliberation and action.[15]

The new and basic ecumenical insight, therefore, is that
among the baptized, there already exists a fundamental unity or
communio, so that the distinction is not between full unity and no
unity, but between full and incomplete *communio*.[16]

The concept of *communio*, however, can hold different meanings and call forth different expectations and projected goals, resulting in mixed messages and frustration. In a secularized setting, it
can refer to an association of free and equal partners in community.
In a church setting, it can be understood as common participation
in the trinitarian life through baptism and Eucharist. In this setting,
there is both a vertical and a horizontal dimension of communion.
Through sharing in the Eucharistic body, we become an ecclesial
body. Consistent with all we have said above about the ecumenical
conviction and the ecumenical indicative, the *communio* does not
come about by gathering individuals into a community. Rather,
individual people are incorporated into the sacramentally given
communion, and the sacramental communion expresses itself in
communal and social behavior.[17]

While there is an emerging agreement on this concept of
koinonia/communio, different emphases can be placed on different
aspects of it, resulting in different and sometimes even opposing
communio-ecclesiologies. Thus, the ecumenical goal, accepted today

by most of the churches stemming from the Reformation, is not institutional unity or organic union, as suggested at New Delhi, but conciliar fellowship (as underlies the Leuenberg Church Fellowship of 1973 or as proposed at the WCC Assembly in Nairobi in 1975)—a communion of churches that remain independent but recognize each other as churches and agree to have altar and pulpit fellowship as well as mutually accepted ministries and services.

The question remains how the Reformation model of unity, as a network of confessional families of churches, is compatible with the Catholic ecclesiological approach. Full communion in the Catholic understanding entails 1) agreement in the apostolic faith; 2) sharing the same sacraments; 3) communion among the churches, which is maintained by the communion among their bishops, and with their head, the bishop of Rome. Some progress has been made in formulating the problem, and possible lines of convergence are beginning to appear, but so far, an ecumenical consensus is not in sight as to what kind of boat would serve us best for the journey.[18]

Orthodox Metropolitan John Zizioulas has trenchantly declared that we must all be ready to undergo sacrifices for the sake of the unity of the Church.

> All confessional identities will have to sacrifice something of their cultural heritage for the sake of unity. They should even go as far as giving up confessionalism altogether for the sake of the emergence of the local Churches truly and visibly united. The model of peaceful and amicable co-existence of our confessions may appeal to most of us as the nicest and easiest solution of the ecumenical problem, since it involves practically no sacrifice by anyone. It can be described as diversity rather than unity.
>
> Equally, the model of organic absorption of all confessions by one particular confessional family would amount to a unity without diversity, a totalitarian kind of unity. Only a unity that results from constantly placing

our confessional particularities in the light of the Kingdom of God, critically as well as positively, to the existential needs of the world can form a health basis for ecumenism.[19]

Zizioulas describes a situation in which visible unity has been replaced by peaceful coexistence and friendly cooperation, and full communion has been replaced by occasional intercommunion. We must not blur the fundamental difference between legitimate diversity in the expression of the faith, on the one hand, and the contradiction between opposite positions, on the other. It is not a so-called union of churches without real unity that we seek, but a truly reconciled diversity.

For many post-modern believers, church union spontaneously seems to imply the loss of particular identities. They prefer pluralism and diversity to unity. But when one looks at the very diverse family of united churches, it becomes clear that the term "organic unity" is used, not to impose uniformity, but precisely to guard the diversity and distinctive gifts of the churches coming together into union.[20]

Nonetheless, the WCC's benchmark New Delhi statement declares, "the achievement of unity will involve nothing less than the death and rebirth of many forms of church life as we have known them. We believe that nothing less costly can finally suffice."[21]

The future agenda of the ecumenical movement will have to address the question of the kind of structure necessary to express the unity of all Christians at the local and universal level.

Stay Motivated: Tightening the Connection Between Ecumenism and Evangelism

We must recover a clear sense that *unity is for mission.*

The commonly cited birthplace of the modern ecumenical movement was the Edinburgh (Scotland) World Missionary Conference in 1910. At that event, evangelism and ecumenism were intrinsically linked. The missionaries, working in the different countries of the world, had painful experience that the divisions amongst themselves were a stumbling block to the gospel of reconciliation to which they sought to give witness.

As we have already noted, this stands in sharp contrast to the situation today. Those churches that place a strong emphasis on evangelism are generally not very enthusiastic about ecumenism. Much of the growth in conversions to Christianity throughout the world is taking place in churches that have only loose association (if that) with an official denominational body. We are witnessing the "third wave" in the history of Christianity in the spread of Pentecostals and charismatics who, with about 500 million faithful worldwide,[22] are now the second largest confessional family whose growth continues to be exponential.

On the other hand, those who tend to affirm ecumenism often tend to avoid aggressive evangelistic efforts. Churches affiliated with the World Council seem inclined to emphasize either social justice concerns or ecumenical agreements on doctrinal subjects—but not explicit missionary activity. In many cases, there are good reasons for this, given inappropriate forms of missionizing activity in contexts such as Latin America or Eastern Europe, where there is already an established church. Questions awaiting a consensus are: What value do we place on missionary activity, especially given our increasing sensibilities to the context of religious pluralism? How should "mission" and "evangelization" be defined; and when is there an appropriate context and when not?[23]

A new ecumenical enthusiasm will only come with a renewed missionary spirit and a theology for the new missionary situation on our own continent.

Follow the Leader:
the Holy Spirit Knows the Way

Biblical scholar Joseph Fitzmeyer observes that the Council of Jerusalem is located smack in the center of the Acts of the

Apostles and indicates a turning point in the story of the early church.[24] It signifies the Church's shift from being centered in Jerusalem to reaching out "to the ends of the earth" (1:8). The apostolic college of Jerusalem officially recognizes the evangelization of the Gentiles, which has been initiated by Peter and carried out on a wide scale by Barnabas and Paul.[25]

At the heart of the missionizing movement from Jerusalem to Judea and Samaria to the ends of the earth is the Holy Spirit, guiding the Church's mission and at the same time, keeping the Gentile Christians in union with the Jewish Christians. The focus of all missionary and ecumenical activity in Acts is the Holy Spirit, and the unity the Spirit brings is, neither a rigid conformity, nor a bland homogeneity.

This Spirit does not efface individual or communal deliberation, but enables it to do what it could not do without the Spirit's power. The Spirit received encourages the new communities, and the individuals within them, to move out in mission, but to do so in communion with one another, acting together for the common good.[26]

Leave Your Ego Behind:
Repentance and Conversion

The imperative of giving visible expression to our unity is driven at its deepest level by the recognition that our disunity is *sin*, born and sustained by many complex social, political, and theological factors to be sure, but rife nonetheless with human sinfulness, both personal and corporate. Thus, did the Catholic bishops at Vatican II state that "such division openly contradicts the will of Christ, scandalizes the world, and damages that most holy cause, the preaching of the Gospel to every creature."[27]

Instead of common witness to the One Lord, what we have is competing denominations. Instead of renewal through the sharing of spiritual gifts, what we have is defensive protection of

119

"our gifts" and agenda. Instead of common work for justice, what we have is separate (and at times contradictory) initiatives. Instead of a community that shows the world an alternative vision of human life, what we have are communities that parrot the surrounding culture's values and visions.[28]

The notion that unity will require repentance is neither novel nor controversial. Penitence involves accepting the disciplines and renunciations necessary to weaken and remove that which is contrary to God's will. Repentance of this sin and its consequences is a necessary condition for progress toward unity. Since God wills that we be one, divided churches must accept the penitential path in obedience to the imperative of unity.

"There can be no ecumenism worthy of the name," said the Catholic bishops at the Second Vatican Council, "without interior conversion. For it is from newness of attitudes of mind, from self-denial and unstinted love, that desires for unity take their rise and develop in a mature way. We should therefore pray to the Holy Spirit for the grace to be genuinely self-denying, humble, gentle in the service of others, and to have an attitude of brotherly [and sisterly] generosity toward them."[29]

Bring Along a Sturdy Repair Kit: Reform

Foremost among our penitential obligations is the constant reform of the Church itself. Catholics were told by their bishops at Vatican II that, in ecumenical work, they must be concerned for members of other churches, initiate relationships, and pray for them, "but their primary duty is to make a careful and honest appraisal of whatever needs to be renewed and done in the Catholic household itself, in order that its life may bear witness more clearly and faithfully to the teachings and institutions which have been handed down from Christ through the Apostles."[30] The Church is a pilgrim church, a church always purifying itself, and must constantly take the path of penance and renewal.

So let me give but one or two examples of reforms needed

within our own church. Cardinal Walter Kasper, president of the Pontifical Council for Promoting Christian Unity from 2001–2010, publicly stated on more than one occasion that the Roman Catholic Church must overcome her one-sided, monolithic structure and develop more communal, collegial, and synodical structures. Such frameworks of intramural dialogue are a presupposition for extramural dialogue.[31]

As we have seen, ministries in the Church, particularly the episcopate in the apostolic succession and the Petrine ministry, are crucial points in the ecumenical dialogue. While the Catholic Church's conviction is that both are a gift for the Church and could be, in a spiritually renewed form, for the good of all, we Catholics have some valuable things to learn from Anglicans, the Orthodox, and Reformation traditions, namely, how best to integrate these ministerial offices within synodical and collegial structures. The effort to develop and strengthen these structures within our own church is the only way forward that holds a realistic hope of reaching an ecumenical consensus on ministries in the Church.[32]

Many churches, stemming from the Reformation, have already joined together to form worldwide confessional associations. With this new openness to a more universalist viewpoint, the question of the possibility of a universal ministry of unity has been raised in several dialogues. Despite this new openness, a basic consensus is still not in view. While the ecumenically open positions of the other churches may consider such a ministry of unity to be *possible*—and maybe even *desirable*—they do not recognize it as *essential* for the Church.

In the meantime, work goes forward to base the ministry of Peter on the New Testament Petrine tradition—not as a dominant power, but as a service of love, a pastoral service after the example of Jesus, the good shepherd, who gives his life for his flock (John 10:11). In his encyclical, *That All May Be One*, Pope John Paul II invited input from other churches as to how the Petrine office could be rendered acceptable to them without stripping it of its essential features.[33] Cardinal Kasper reported, "We got a huge number of official and non-official answers, which we collected and analyzed carefully. Without doubt, they indicate a new climate and a new openness; they show some convergences, but up to now, no consensus can be found. Most of the churches and church communities want communion *with* Peter but no communion *under* Peter."[34]

Vatican II itself called for the Petrine ministry to be integrated into the whole constellation of the Church and interpreted as a service to the communion of the faithful, as a ministry of oversight, a keeping watch like a sentinel to safeguard unity in the truth in the life of the Church. The three dimensions called for by the WCC's Faith and Order Commission as essential for every ministry would also apply to this ministry: it has to be exercised in a personal, collegial, and communal way.[35]

At the same time, pastoral responsibility without the means to execute it would not help the Church in the urgent situations where she most needs it, so a "primacy of honor" in a merely honorific sense would not do either, to say nothing of being against the spirit of the Gospel ("I have come not to be served, but to serve"). Thus, a primacy of jurisdiction cannot be opposed to a pastoral primacy of service. John Paul II referred to the martyr–bishop Ignatius of Antioch, who described the primacy of Rome as the "primacy of love." His interpretation is not one of jurisdiction based on the idea of sovereignty, but a spiritual one based on the idea of service—a service to unity, service and sign of mercy and love.[36]

At the very least, we can say that the old controversy has been replaced by a new openness. In the 2007 Ravenna Document, unanimously approved by the members of the Joint International Commission for the Theological Dialogue between the Roman Catholic Church and the Orthodox Church, the primacy of the bishop of Rome is recognized.[37] Another noteworthy sign of progress was the 2010 statement by the North American Orthodox-Catholic Theological Consultation entitled "Steps Towards A Reunited Church: A Sketch of an Orthodox-Catholic Vision for the Future." In it, the commission members state: "It is urgent that Orthodox and Catholic Christians find an effective way to realize our common tradition of faith together, and to present the world with a unified testimony to the Lordship of Jesus. To be what we are called to be, we need each other....To become what we are...we cannot stop short of re-establishing full Eucharistic communion among ourselves."[38]

After 950 years of division between us, the language is now that "it is *urgent*" to put an end to this. One might say that, thanks to prayer, local action, and the work of commissions like this, there's been a sea change. Consultation members do not shy from addressing the hard issues head-on and recognize that this cannot be achieved without "new, better harmonized structures of leadership on both sides: new conceptions of both synodality and primacy in the universal Church, new approaches to the way authority and primacy are exercised in both our communions."[39]

What is encouraging about the Consultation's statement is that they have reached the stage where they are imagining, in concrete terms, what it would look like to be in full communion with one another. This means that reconciliation—full communion—between the Latin, Eastern Catholic, and Eastern Orthodox Churches is closer than it has ever been before.

In our new context of a globalized world, the idea that there might be a ministry of unity in the Church is receiving fresh consideration ecumenically. This is accompanied, on the Catholic side, by the growing conviction that a spiritual and institutional renewal within the Catholic Church is fundamental for any future ecumenical understanding. These are the new prerequisites for a theological discussion on the question of the Petrine ministry.[40]

Everybody Paddles: Receptive Ecumenism

While commitment to hope and work for structural unification continue to represent core Catholic instincts, it is nonetheless clear that realizing it in actual terms will be a marathon run. The answer in the situation is not to tire and move toward a lesser goal of "reconciled diversity without structural unity," but rather to envision how Christian traditions might more genuinely and effectively learn or receive from one another with integrity *now*.

One international conference was held in Durham, England, in 2006 and a second in 2009, emphasizing a strategy called Receptive Ecumenism. Encouraged is an approach that is both realistic in the face of current difficulties and, at the same time, imaginative and bold. How are we to live in the interim, not giving up on the vision; not tempted to settle for less? How might we learn and receive from one another in this middle time, with its challenges and problems?[41]

Required is a fundamental shift from each tradition of Christian faith assertively defending its own perceived inheritance in competition with each other, to taking responsibility for its own potential learning from others. For this process of overcoming our historical defensive postures to begin, some have to take responsibility, to take the initiative—regardless of whether others are ready to reciprocate. As the therapeutic adage goes: "We cannot change others. We can only change ourselves and, thereby, the way we relate to others. But doing this will itself alter things and open up new possibilities."[42]

Similarly, each tradition is, in turn, willing to facilitate the learning of others as requested, but without either requiring how this should be done, and without making this a precondition to attending to one's own learning. In short, learning will take precedence over teaching.[43]

Receptive Ecumenism is about coming to a positive appreciation for the presence and action of God in the people, practices, structures, and processes of another tradition and being impelled, thereby, to search for ways in which all impediments to our closer relationship might be overcome. This does not result in our becoming *less* Catholic but in our becoming *more* Catholic precisely by expanding our possibilities and stimulating the process of ecclesial growth and conversion. The gospel calls us to greater life and flourishing.[44]

Sometimes people conceive of reconciliation among Christians in lowest-common-denominator terms and resist it, because they fear it will result in the loss of their tradition's distinctive richness. It must be clearly understood that Receptive Ecumenism is about the intensification and further realization of Catholic identity, not its diminishment and loss. It is an authentically Catholic instinct always to seek the truth potentially to be learned from the "other"—with due discernment, criticism, and appropriate concern for integrity intact.[45]

Receptive Ecumenism seeks to cultivate within us the *necessary prior desire* for deeper relationship with other Christians that the formal dialogues between our churches presuppose and without which their work will never come to fruition. That necessary prior desire is the work of the Holy Spirit, an inclination of our hearts that finds delight in another's gifts and beauties, that is able to recognize a fitting match between our particular lacks and needs and the other's particular gifts.[46]

Ongoing conversion opens us up to the possibility that, within each of our traditions, we can become more sharply aware of our own respective lacks, needs, and sticking points, and of our inability to attend to them, of our own resources without recourse to the particular gifts of other traditions. This is the kind of real ecumenical learning that will move us closer to finding ourselves in the other, the other in ourselves, and each in Christ.[47]

So the questions are: What might we have to learn from other Christian traditions? And what might be the factors militating against such potential learning, and how might we best negotiate them?

The personal and relational are always prior to the structural and institutional. Journeying out of our isolations, meeting, getting to know and trust one another, and establishing friendships form the climate in which separated communities become open to receiving gifts from each other. It is the climate out of which a passion for unity is born and sustained. Symbolic gestures are important between church leaders, but relationships of trust and mutual affection have to grow as well between members of different churches if reconciliation is to happen.

It was not by accident that we began this chapter by observing that "reconciliation," in its Greek utilization in biblical times, was the term normally used for the resumption of common life between husband and wife. In other words, the Church is the community of those who, because of Christ, are no longer separated. Reconciliation and unity are of the very nature of the Church of Christ. To be "in communion of life" with one another as Christians is our vocation.

Notes

1. Alan Richardson, ed., *A Theological Word Book of the Bible* (New York: Macmillan, 1950), 184.

2. W. E. Vine, M. F. Unger, and W. White Jr., *Vine's Complete Expository Dictionary of Old and New Testament Words* (Atlanta: Thomas Nelson Publisher, 1985), 514. See, for example, 2 Cor 5:19; Rom 5:10; Col 1:13–14; Eph 2:18.

3. Aram I, "Report of the Moderator," in *God in Your Grace: Official Report of the Ninth Assembly of the World Council of Churches*, ed. Luis N. Rivera-Pagán (Geneva: WCC Publications, 2007), 122–35.

4. Ibid., 120–21.

5. In Michael Kinnamon and Brian E. Cope, eds., *The Ecumenical Movement: An Anthology of Key Texts and Voices* (Geneva: WCC; Grand Rapids, MI: Eerdmans, 1997), 469.

6. *Ut Unum Sint: On Commitment to Ecumenism* (Boston: Pauline Books and Media, 1995), 77.

7. Ibid., 88.

8. "Call to be the One Church: Text on Ecclesiology," in *God in Your Grace*, 265–67.

9. Kinnamon and Cope, *Ecumenical Movement*, 466.

10. See for example in *The Decree on Ecumenism*, par. 17, 19, 22.

11. As quoted in Michael Kinnamon, *The Vision of the Ecumenical Movement and How It Has Been Impoverished by Its Friends* (St. Louis, MO: Chalice Press, 2003), 10.

12. Kinnamon, *Vision*, 17, 22.

13. Cardinal Walter Kasper in a keynote address to the National Workshop on Christian Unity, Cleveland, Ohio, May 17, 2002.

14. Walter Kasper, *That They May All Be One* (London: Burns & Oats, 2004), 58.

15. Kinnamon and Cope, *Ecumenical Movement*, 124.

16. Kasper, *That They May All Be One*, 51.

17. Ibid., 58–59.

18. Ibid., 63–64.

19. As quoted in Peter De Mey, "A Call to Conversion: An Analysis of *The Princeton Proposal for Christian Unity* (2003)," *Ecumenical Trends*, vol. 34, no. 4 (April 2005): 253.

20. T. F. Best, "Church Union: An Answer to Its Post-Modern Despisers," *The Ecumenical Review* 56 (2004): 118–127.

21. Kinnamon and Cope, *Ecumenical Movement*, 89.

22. http://en.wikipedia.org/wiki/Pentecostalism, accessed June 25, 2011.

23. Lois Malcolm, "'It Has Seemed Good to the Holy Spirit and to Us': Mission and Ecumenism in the Power of the Holy Spirit," in *The Ecumenical Future*, ed. Carl E. Braaten and Robert W. Jenson, 220 (Grand Rapids, MI: W.B. Eerdmans, 2004).

24. Ibid., 222.

25. Ibid., 226.

26. Ibid., 232, 234.

27. "The Decree on Ecumenism," in *The Documents of Vatican II*, ed. Walter Abbott, SJ, 340 (The America Press, 1966).

28. Kinnamon, *Vision*, 31.

29. "The Decree on Ecumenism," 351, par. 7.

30. Ibid., 348, par. 4.

31. Kasper, *That They May All Be One*, 42.

32. Ibid., 74. With reference to the Petrine Ministry, the issue is to disentangle the functions that have accrued to the papacy in the course of time. The essential and indispensable duties of Petrine ministry need to be distinguished from those duties that pertain to the pope as the first bishop of the Latin Church (patriarch), and from those duties that have accrued over time. Such a distinction could also lead to consequences for the structuring of the Roman Catholic Church (Kasper, 83).

33. John Paul II, *Ut Unum Sint*, 1995, par. 96; *Origins*, vol. 25, no. 4 (June 8, 1995), 70: "This is an immense task, which we cannot refuse and which I cannot carry out by myself. Could not the real but imperfect communion existing between us persuade church leaders and their theologians to engage with me in a patient and fraternal dialogue on this subject, a dialogue which, leaving useless controversies behind, we could listen to one another, keeping before us only the will of Christ for his church and allowing ourselves to be deeply moved by his pleas 'that they may all be one...so that the world may believe that you have sent me' (John 17:21)."

34. Cardinal Kasper, in an address to the National Workshop on Christian Unity in Cleveland, Ohio, May 17, 2002.

35. *Baptism, Eucharist, and Ministry*, Faith and Order Paper no. 111 (World Council of Churches, Geneva: 1982), "Ministry," par. 26.

36. Kasper, *That They May All Be One*, 148.

37. Joint International Commission for the Theological Dialogue Between the Roman Catholic and the Orthodox Church, "Ecclesiological and Canonical Consequences of the Sacramental Nature of the Church: Ecclesial Communion, Conciliarity and Authority," *The Ravenna Document* (Ravenna, Italy, October 13, 2007). "Both sides agree...that Rome, as the Church that "presides in love" according to the phrase of St Ignatius of Antioch (*To the Romans*, Prologue), occupied the first place in the *taxis* (canonical order), and that the bishop of Rome was therefore the *protos* (first) among the patriarchs. They disagree, however, on the interpretation of the historical evidence from this era regarding the prerogatives of the bishop of Rome as *protos*, a matter that was already understood in different ways in the first millennium" (par. 41).

38. The North American Orthodox-Catholic Theological Consultation, "Steps Towards a Reunited Church: A Sketch of an Orthodox-Catholic Vision for the Future" (Georgetown University, Washington, DC, October 2, 2010), par. 5.

39. Ibid.

40. Kasper, *That They May All Be One*, 139.

41. Mary Tanner, "From Vatican II to Missauga—Lessons in Receptive Ecumenical Learning from the A-RC Bilateral Dialogue Process," in *Receptive Ecumenism and the Call to Catholic Learning: Exploring a Way for Contemporary Ecumenism*, ed. Paul Murray, 258 (Oxford University Press, 2008).

42. Paul Murray, "Receptive Ecumenism and Catholic Learning—Establishing the Agenda, in *Receptive Ecumenism and the Call to Catholic Learning: Exploring a Way for Contemporary Ecumenism*, ed. Paul Murray, 15 (Oxford University Press, 2008).

43. Ibid.

44. Ibid., 16.

45. Ibid., 17.

46. Ibid., 16.

47. Ibid.

9

HEALING AND FORGIVENESS: AN INTERFAITH PERSPECTIVE

Rodney L. Petersen

Introduction

Many persons are familiar with the story of Jesus' healing of the paralytic, the account of which is found in the Gospel of Mark. You might remember that the event elicits criticism from the authorities, who accuse Jesus of blasphemy. Rather than at first healing the man, Jesus forgives him his sins. Jesus is criticized by those identified as Pharisees for doing something only God can do, that is, forgive sins. As the story continues, Jesus responds to those who criticize him by "downgrading" his remarks: He simply tells the paralytic, "...stand up, take your mat and go to your home" (2:11). But he does this without, for a minute, retracting the connection between healing and forgiveness.

> A few days later, when Jesus again entered Capernaum, the people heard that he had come home. They gathered in such large numbers that there was no room left, not even outside the door, and he preached the word to them. Some men came, bringing to him a paralyzed man, carried by four of them. Since they could not get him to Jesus because of the crowd, they made an open-

ing in the roof above Jesus by digging through it and then lowered the mat the man was lying on. When Jesus saw their faith, he said to the paralyzed man, "Son, your sins are forgiven." (Mark 2:1-5 and see 6-12; NIV)

The relation between healing, forgiveness, and religion is grounded in an understanding of health and human wholeness. Every Christian tradition has prayers and pieties associated with healing, forgiveness, and faith. In Catholicism alone, more than six million people travel each year to the shrine at Lourdes in France to ask for healing and forgiveness. Among Orthodox Christians, St. John Chrysostom writes of the Church as a physician, sin as an illness, and forgiveness as a journey toward healing and health. Protestants, who participate in the same grand narrative as Roman Catholics and Orthodox believers, hold that they are saved by God's forgiving grace, a grace that leads to health and human wholeness. In addition, in Boston (USA) there is even a denomination with international reach founded upon this relationship, Christian Science, or The First Church of Christ, Scientist.

Christianity is not alone in associating healing, forgiveness, and religion. Every expression of religion, for example, the Abrahamic traditions, Indic religions and practices, and aboriginal and indigenous religion, associates faith, forgiveness, and health. In this article, we will consider the relation between healing and religion and, then, take up the question of the relation between healing and forgiveness. Finally, we shall consider several of the major world religions, asking what they offer by way of healing through forgiveness.

Healing and Religion

The value of religion for health and healing lays, first of all, in the ways religion offers orientation in the world, important for psychic health. Sigmund Freud put this most clearly in relation to his work on world views and how such function for the human psyche. According to Freud, the value of a worldview is that, through it, we gain access to knowledge about our identity or origins, find direction in life and consolation in the face of life's inevitable setbacks. Religion "frames" meaning; it provides a narrative for life. Although Freud rejected religion as he knew it, believing that he found, in science, a better world view, its function along with philosophy, art, and aesthetics remained. Freud described a world view, or *Weltanschauung*, as "an intellectual construction which solves all the problems of our existence uniformly on the basis of one overriding hypothesis...."[1] Accordingly, for Freud, the sciences overtook other competitors to defining an appropriate "worldview."[2]

The point is that a worldview, most often a religious worldview, offers consolation and a way to put the world together in the face of trauma and the violence of life. Consolation relates to the deep meaning of religion, the origins of psychoanalytic studies, and to health and human wholeness. It bears directly upon our theme for this volume, *Healing God's People: Practical Skills and Pastoral Approaches*. With some sense of irony, the very idea of consolation strikes at the heart of Freud's work as he surrounded himself in his study with the symbols and fetishes of almost every known religion while pursuing his ground-breaking work in the psychoanalytic sciences. This very fact, drawn from the biography of Freud's life, draws us to our connection between health and human wholeness.

Religion can also offer healing and health to group consciousness, even to the life of a nation. The very origins of sociology find religion to be an extremely important variable for social health. The sociologist Emile Durkheim studied the role of religion in society. Working as a positivist, he distinguished between the social function of religion and the philosophy of religion, or theology, to separate from an assessment of the validity of religious beliefs. In his foundational work, he noted the connection between the social function of religion to offer meaning and integration in society and individual social health.[3] Other sociologists—such as, Karl Marx and Max Weber—would take up the question of religion's role differently, some finding religion's contribution to healing more troublesome than helpful. In his philosophical assessment of religion, Rudolf Otto found in the idea of the holy, the *mysterium tremendum*, a powerful and nonrational idea that was beyond moral interpretation.[4] This idea, as related to religion's power as a force for good or ill, became the impetus for the work of Scott Appleby and peace-building as he sought to construct such out of the positive force for good that religion could offer.[5]

The political philosopher of the post-World War II period, Hannah Arendt, located this force for good in religion in the idea of forgiveness—that through forgiveness, societies and persons in distress could find their way back to social healing. It is a connection that led Arendt even to contend that Jesus was the author of forgiveness, finding the idea of forgiveness so deeply wed to Jesus' ministry.[6] The significance given this by Arendt is that through forgiveness we are able to start again, to find renewal and a new sense of meaning in relationships, circumstances, and the affairs of life. Arendt related this function of forgiveness, not only to the individual, but also to social health in the aftermath of the Second World War.[7] Religion is more than consolation. It is about meaning-making. We are most at loss with our sense of meaning in the face of violence and its causes.[8]

Healing and Forgiveness

If we can establish a relation between healing and religion, what might now be said about healing and forgiveness? In the story that began this paper, Jesus connects an understanding of health with forgiveness, forgiveness related to the healing of persons. The links between healing and forgiveness become further intertwined in the face of unhealed trauma and cycles of violence. Psychological research increasingly illustrates the processes involved in forgiveness.[9] Prior to the 1980s, forgiveness was a practice primarily left to matters of faith. Over the past quarter century, psychological research has concluded that forgiveness is a process. A number of models, describing the process of forgiveness, have been published, including one from a radical behavioral perspective.[10]

For example, Robert Enright of the University of Wisconsin–Madison founded the International Forgiveness Institute and is considered the initiator of forgiveness studies. He developed a twenty-step Process Model of Forgiveness.[11] Recent work has focused on what kind of person is more likely to be forgiving. A longitudinal study showed that people who were generally more angry and hostile in life were less likely to forgive another person, even after a long time had passed. Specifically, these people were more likely to still avoid their transgressor and want to enact revenge upon them two and a half years after the transgression.[12]

Psychologist Everett L. Worthington has studied the motivations that reduce interactions with one who has hurt us as related to forgiveness and health.[13] Another researcher from the University of Wisconsin, working on a program on forgiveness with Robert Enright, Joanna North writes, "Forgiveness is a matter of a willed change of heart, the successful result of an active endeavor to replace bad thoughts with good, bitterness and anger with compassion and affection." Participation in a religious community can give the courage to make those steps, which may begin in only a detached and limited fashion along a road toward healing individual and social health.[14]

Unprocessed trauma results in physical and/or emotional (and spiritual) hyper-alertness. The lower brain remains vigilant, always looking for the enemy in order to keep ourselves safe. Events and people are quickly given a "threat" interpretation. This is part of what is called "acting out" reenactment. Acting out, turning unhealed pain energy out onto others, is often seen in child abuse; the inability to be flexible, tolerant, and show empathy to others; participation in high-risk behaviors; and in difficulty in intimate relations (e.g., domestic abuse, blaming, irritability). At the macro level, this is perhaps seen in repetitive conflicts and wars. On the other hand, acting in—or the turning of unhealed pain energy in on oneself—is frequently seen in alcohol and drug abuse, overwork, eating too much or too little, depression, numbness, anxiety, self-blame, shame, self-mutilation, and in such physical symptoms as high blood pressure, pain (chest, back, joints), headaches, and digestive problems.

Studies show that people who forgive are happier and healthier than those who hold resentments.[15] The first study to look at how forgiveness improves physical health discovered that, when people think about forgiving an offender, it leads to improved functioning in their cardiovascular and nervous systems.[16] Another study at the University of Wisconsin found that the more forgiving people were, the less they suffered from a wide range of illnesses. The less-forgiving people reported a greater number of health problems.[17] A traumatic event or act of aggression leaves an emotional lesion on our life, the effects of such trauma wounds the spirit. It can have physiological, psychosocial, and spiritual effects, with implications for individuals, but also for communities and societies.

To understand something of the complexity here, we need to understand our own psychosocial and physiological complexity of body—the need to construct meaning and impact of unmet needs. Our brain, which controls our body, is composed of three parts: the instinctual brain, associated with the brain stem; emotional brain or limbic system; and the rational brain or cerebral cortex. For the instinctual brain, or brain stem, everything is now; it is concerned about self-preservation, about asking: "Is this situation safe? Is it something to nurture or be nurtured by, to run away from (flight), to attack (fight), to submit to (freeze)." It is a nexus of automatic reactions reflected in reproduction, blood circulation, muscle contraction, temperature regulation, breathing, and sleeping. This is different from the emotional brain, which resides in the limbic system, the site of emotions, of memory storage, and of automatic reactions. This is the "first alert" alarm system in times of stress and crisis. Then, there is the rational brain, the site of our cognitive (thinking) functions. Here, there is a sense of linear time (yesterday, today, tomorrow). Conscious and alert, we are oriented to observations, anticipation, planning, and responding. This is the origin of our organization of information and decision-making processes. Here is where our logic resides and it is the ideational center of our lives.[18]

Trauma *disorders* the orbital frontal cortex functioning. Its normal functions are to register sensations, connect through non-verbal communication, and regulate the emotions. It is a part of response flexibility (the ability to take in input from the inside and outside world, to pause and be mindful, to think about and choose the most appropriate option: flexibility). It works for social cognition (ability to have empathy), autobiographical memory and narrative (self-knowing awareness), the extinction of fear, and helps to regulate morality, being moral, treating people with kindness, and doing well. Under normal conditions, the thinking brain immediately can influence reactions of the emotional and instinctual brains. However, in high-anxiety situations, the rational brain is "the last to know." During times of high stress and crisis, memories and emotions are not processed and stored in the normal way. The lower brain doesn't know the crisis is over. What happens to all the extra energy (hyper-arousal) generated in the body in response to stress or trauma? If not released, the frozen or un-used energy is trapped in the body (brain, nervous system, muscles) where it wreaks havoc on our bodies in the form of stress or trauma reactions.[19]

According to Psychologist Andrew Newberg, the mechanism of forgiveness developed as an evolutionary adaptation out of an instinctive need for self-preservation, the latter being precognitive. His definition of forgiveness is the forgoing of retaliation after being wronged. Worthington understands the cure as a process of de-conditioning, which has five steps: recalling the traumatic event (habituating), empathizing with the perpetrator, forgiveness, a public commitment to forgiveness, and perseverance. The last two steps are necessary because de-conditioning is the process of breaking a habit; to break the habit, a public commitment is helpful and perseverance in forgiving again and again is necessary. The research of Frederic Luskin of Stanford University shows that forgiveness can be learned.[20]

Finally, we might add that *forgiveness* and *reconciliation* are not the same.[21] Worthington shows that they can occur together, but this is not necessarily the case. Forgiveness can be understood as an individual act or inner reorientation. Even though a perpetrator can ask for forgiveness, the initiative is on the side of the victim. Forgiveness can even be granted if the perpetrator is no longer available, for instance, because he or she has died. Reconciliation, on the other hand, is always part and parcel of a relation. In order for reconciliation to take place, perpetrator and victim have to interact and go through a process. This process is meant to restore the relation that existed between the two parties and was violated by the wrong committed. In order for the process to be successful, the perpetrator has to perform some form of *atonement*.[22]

Healing also comes by finding oneself in a stronger narrative than that dictated by an abuse. Forgiveness is the process that enables healing to happen; it does not necessarily offer the definitions of that larger narrative. Among various competitors for that stronger narrative, religion offers such but not necessarily with one voice. Different wisdom traditions, set in different frameworks for understanding the world, offer different nuances to the concept of forgiveness that can help social scientists appreciate the impact of different religious conceptualizations—and can help health professionals discern different roads to healing. The idea of forgiveness is not a monolithic concept. Social scientists, but also theologians and practitioners of religion, who appreciate the contributions of different religious perspectives on forgiveness, can have greater success with the personal and social healing that can accompany forgiveness.[23] Different traditions of a religious expression have contextualized and defined forgiveness differently. Such different conceptions of forgiveness bear upon the research and practice of forgiveness and upon pastoral skills and practical approaches to healing in an endeavor to heal God's people.

Healing and Forgiveness: An Inter-Faith Perspective

Most world religions include teachings on the nature of forgiveness, and many of these teachings provide an underlying basis for the varying traditions and practices of forgiveness as a means toward health and healing in their community life. In order to better understand religious contributions to forgiveness in light of heightened social and research interests, we might divide the religions of the world into three broad categories: the Abrahamic family of religions, the Indic religions, and aboriginal beliefs and practices, each offering different skills and pastoral approaches. While this division is not inclusive and lends itself as much to overgeneralization as to clarity, it will nevertheless be helpful as we seek to understand a practice that has been said to be a hard-wired aspect of human nature.[24] And, we might tease out of each of these broad traditions different aspects of healing and health related to ways in which forgiveness is nuanced differently.

Abrahamic Family

Forgiveness functions in important—if also in different—ways in the Abrahamic family of religions: in Judaism, Christianity, and in Islam. For each of these three faiths, forgiveness is worked out in the context of historical events that open up new perspectives, it relates to the maturation of personal relationships, and it is shaped by an understanding of God—the ontological grounding for the human personality and of faith, the very structure of understanding that is monotheistic, transcendent, and capable of an immanent relationship with human personality. The nature of one's relationships with others, who also are made in the image of God, is said to be illustrative of one's relationship with God. While differences

138

exist, there are deep affinities in these three faith traditions as illustrated in their scriptures.[25]

JUDAISM

Jews observe a Day of Atonement, Yom Kippur, on which occasion they ask forgiveness of those they have wronged if they have not already done so. God forgives one for the sins one has committed against God, but it is necessary for Jews also to seek the forgiveness of those people whom they have wronged. In Judaism, if a person causes harm, but then sincerely and honestly apologizes to the wronged individual and tries to rectify the wrong, the wronged individual is religiously required to grant forgiveness. In Judaism, one must go to those he has harmed in order to be entitled to forgiveness.[26] Thus, the "reward" for forgiving others is not God's forgiveness for wrongs done to others, but rather help in obtaining forgiveness from the other person.[27]

The story of Joseph's encounter with his brothers (Gen/ Breishit 50:19–21), the forgiveness he offers them for having sold him into slavery and all that ensues, is paradigmatic for Judaism. At least four important lessons are laid out here that govern Jewish concerns about the legitimacy of forgiveness. First, Joseph grounds his understanding of forgiveness in his conception of God. In other words, the basis for forgiveness is in imitation of God. "Am I in the place of God? You intended to harm me, but God intended it for good...." Second, it is the victim who usually begins the process of forgiveness. Third, the demands for justice are specific if there is to be restoration. This is seen in Joseph's earlier encounters with his brothers as they seek his assistance in the context of the famine in the land. (A concern for the demands of justice is even clearer in the story of Jacob's encounter with Esau after Jacob's earlier deception of their father and theft of Esau's birthright.) Fourth, the end sought is the repair of relationships, evident in Joseph's extension of aid to his brothers and to their progeny.[28]

To fast forward several millennia, this concern among persons understood to have been created in God's image for justice toward repair of relationship, remains central for Judaism. In contemporary history this has caused no end of anxiety and conscious self-reflection.[29] Taking his cue from the book, *The Sunflower*,[30] in which Simon Wiesenthal asks Jewish and Christian scholars for their thoughts on his denial of forgiveness to a young, dying SS officer, Solomon Schimmel revisits Wiesenthal's anguished questions by taking seriously perspectives and resources from Judaism, Christianity and Islam. Schimmel draws out the moral ambiguities with which all three traditions grapple among concepts of forgiveness, repentance and reconciliation, laying clear stress on Judaism's concern for personal responsibility, accountability and justice. Using biblical and Talmudic texts, Schimmel draws out the value of his tradition for topics of revenge and justice; for why, when and to whom one should forgive, offer repentance, and seek reconciliation. Reflecting his own tradition's keen interest in justice, he questions other traditions, such as Christianity, that may move too quickly to forgiveness. It is clear, however, that the duty to forgive is central to the Jewish tradition.[31]

CHRISTIANITY

For Christians, the parable of the prodigal son (Luke 15:11–32) is as symbolic as the story of Joseph is for Judaism. Jesus tells the story of a man who has two sons. The younger demands his share of his inheritance while his father is still living, and goes off to a distant country where he "squander[s] his property in dissolute living," and eventually has to take work as a swineherd, whereby, he comes to his senses, decides to return home, and throws himself on his father's mercy, thinking that even if his father does disown him, that being one of his servants is still far better than feeding pigs. The father, representative of the tradition's understanding of God, forgives and restores.[32]

If forgiveness is closely linked with justice in contemporary Jewish thinking, the proximate linkage in Christianity is with another Jewish term, *hesed*, implying unmerited grace. The emotional power of the parable of the prodigal son comes from the unexpected forgiveness of the father (Luke 15:11–32). Similarly, the twist in the parable of the Good Samaritan is that the person who was not obliged to give anything, gave all (Luke 10:30–37). The story of Christianity is that, through the incarnation of God in Jesus, *hesed* was at last perfectly defined in that God takes upon God's self (through the person of Jesus) humanity's injustice, as described in various theories of the atonement.[33] In other words, whereas in Judaism there is a sharpened concern for the law and its use in ferreting out questions of right relationship, this is taken up in Christianity in its theology of the cross, whereby the forgiveness offered humanity releases persons from captivity to the past. Jesus is the sacrificial lamb and image of the Father mediated to humanity. Through Jesus, humanity is taught that, as we forgive, we are forgiven—a theme central to the dominant prayer, the Lord's Prayer (Matt 6:9–15), of the tradition.

The idea of forgiveness frames other aspects of Christianity. The late fourth-century collection of books, known as the *Apostolic Constitutions*, purported to be the work of the twelve apostles, guide clergy and laity in the basics of early Christian discipline, worship, and doctrine. The books are replete with themes of forgiveness as linked to repentance, mercy, and compassion.[34] But how to make forgiveness real has often divided Christian churches. The canons and commentaries of the Orthodox churches, known as the *Pedalion* ("The Rudder"), are seen as guidelines rather than laws. Whereas the Latin and Western Church has tended to be more prescriptive in the ways of law and grace, a medieval conflict, which would come to a head in the Protestant Reformation as the Western Church, would be challenged by reformer Martin Luther's conception of *sola gratia* (salvation, hence forgiveness, by grace alone).

Through its emphasis upon the grace of God in Jesus, Christianity carries seeds of its own revolutionary character, while becoming susceptible to a cheap notion of forgiveness, its triteness, and its inconsequentiality. Seen from the perspective of the sacrifice it entails, "forgiveness" is profound and signals an understanding of sacrifice, which begins with the self-sacrifice of God and is finally met as human beings respond to love with love, overcoming through forgiveness. This self-giving sense of forgiveness defines the nature of the Christian community: There is no worship apart from forgiveness (Matt 5:23–24); forgiveness defines the material identity of the church (John 20:21–23); and forgiveness, as it tends toward reconciliation, defines vocation (2 Cor 5:19).

ISLAM

Islam teaches that God is Al-Ghaffur, "The All-Forgiving", and is the original source of all forgiveness (*ghufran*). Islam does not teach universalism, and the Qur'an states explicitly that God will not forgive idol worship (Qur'an 4:116). Forgiveness often requires the repentance of those being forgiven. Depending on the type of wrong committed, forgiveness can come either directly from Allah, or from one's fellow man who received the wrong (al-Shura 42:37).[35] In the case of divine forgiveness, the asking for divine forgiveness via repentance is important. In the case of human forgiveness, it is important to both forgive and to be forgiven.[36]

The example of the Prophet (PBUH) is central for Islam. The story is told that when he went to Al-Tāif to preach the message of Allah, its people mistreated him. They abused him and hit him with stones. When he took shelter under a tree, the angel of Allah visited him and told him that Allah sent him to destroy the people of Al-Tāif because of their sin of mistreating their Prophet. The Prophet prayed to Allah to save the people of Al-Tāif, because what they did was out of their ignorance. When he entered the city of Makkah after the victory, the Prophet had in front of him some of his staunchest enemies. It is reported that the Prophet asked them, "What do you think I shall do to you now?" They pleaded for mercy. The Prophet said, "Today I shall say to you what Joseph (referring to Prophet Yusuf as mentioned in the *Qur'an*, Yusuf 12:92) said to his brothers, 'No blame on you today.' Go, you are all free." He forgave even Hind, who had caused the murder of his uncle Hamza. After killing him, she had his body mutilated and chewed his liver. When she accepted Islam, the Prophet even forgave her.[37]

Grounding an understanding of forgiveness in the attributes of Allah—that Allah is merciful, forgiving, just, sovereign, and patient—has led to tension in different schools of Islam among those who stress the justice or the mercy of God.[38] While all Muslims agree that Allah forgives and, in the prophet Mohammad (PBUH), finding examples of this; thereby, giving precedent to Islamic leadership in setting an example of such,[39] nevertheless, in the history of Islam, four competing schools of interpretation have developed in an attempt to reconcile the competing claims of the justice and mercy of Allah.[40]

How to live with the tension of justice and mercy has been particularly real in contemporary society, as Muslims have struggled with years of western hegemony and have often turned to the vision of justice in Islam for purposes of identity and even retribution in a post-colonial era, perhaps coming to a head in the Iranian Revolution referred to earlier.[41] God, or Allah, has been drawn into conflict.[42] This is, of course, the case, not only in Islam, but in other settings around the world where issues of politics, economics, and identity have come together, particularly around issues of perceived and real humiliation.[43] In the Islamic tradition, no one has been clearer about the centrality of the mercy and, consequently, forgiveness of God than the controversial Sufi mystic Ibn Arabi for whom such is not only a message of hope, but should be seen in the ethics of godlikeness to which humans must strive.[44]

Indic Religions

The idea and practice of forgiveness among the Indic religions might be considered together. Here, also, significant differences exist among religious perspectives and practices as they have emerged from the Asian subcontinent; nevertheless, Hinduism, Buddhism, and such other faith expressions as Jain religious thought might be considered as dialogic partners around the question of forgiveness. In the contemporary period, Buddhism has been most noted for several outstanding peacemakers, who have worked out a concept of forgiveness in difficult political settings. Buddhism is representative of a general tendency to frame forgiveness by a conception of compassion in a more existential and less theistic fashion, when compared with the Abrahamic traditions.

Hinduism

Hinduism is a diverse and loosely knit collection of cultural and religious practices. Some of these traditions are theistic and some, atheistic; some existential, some metaphysical. The concept of forgiveness is important and often related to a kind of modeling of divinity or a divine pantheon that bears upon success in this life and upon the future insofar as this life is determinative of that future. Evidence for a divine bestowal of forgiveness on human beings reaches back to the Vedic period (c. 5000–1000 BCE) in India. And, despite the wide variety of opinion in Hindu religious understanding, from a sense of the innate peacefulness of their tradition to a defense of holy war, *dharmayudh*, prayers of forgiveness reflecting divine graciousness are prominent in the tradition, and specifically in the Rig-Veda.[45]

A more bellicose interpretation of the tradition, which might seem to mute any interest in forgiveness, can be found in the opening of the Gita in which sacred text begins with a battlefield scene and defense of military honor.[46] This passage illustrates the complexity of Hinduism: While the Aryan (North India) Hindu traditions glorify Rama, some Dravidian (South Indian) traditions give the story an opposite interpretation. The Indian scholar A. K. Ramanujan has stated that there are at least three hundred versions of Ramayana. Whether the tradition is best interpreted through the lens of forgiveness or in a more bellicose fashion can be said to be that which is worked through in the Dharma-Sastras, or law books governing the four castes and stages of life. These books define and work out the implications of sin (*papa*) and atonement (*prayascitta*).

A strong current pulls in the direction of valuing the concept of forgiveness and regarding as allegorical those elements in the tradition that would move in a different direction. Words like *Ksama* or *ksamata*, commonly used in Sanskrit texts to signify forgiveness, are often combined with such words for mercy as *kripa* (or grace), *prasada, daya* (or compassion), and *karuna*.[47] The concept of forgiveness, as discussed in the epics and *dharma sastras* (treatises on righteousness), are such as to encourage following the path of dharma (righteousness). The law of cause and effect (karma) values the virtue of forgiveness, as the consequence of one's actions in this life effect subsequent reincarnation. Writing out of his sense of this complexity, Rajmohan Gandhi writes, "...forgiveness is indeed an issue that Hindus should frontally face. We have harmed fellow Hindus and non-Hindus.... Luckily Hindu tradition upholds forgiveness."[48]

BUDDHISM

The relationship between Hinduism and Buddhism is complex, whether Buddhism is understood to be different from, an offshoot of, or remains a part of Hinduism. What is clear in the contemporary period is that Buddhism has been most noted for several outstanding peacemakers, who have promoted conceptions of forgiveness out of this framework of meaning. For example, since 1988 and the outbreak of the pro-democracy movement, Aung San Suu Kyi, one of the most visible leaders in the nonviolent pro-democracy movement, has worked to connect forgiveness with wisdom through principles of right intention (*cetna*) and compassion (*metta*).[49] Forgiveness is connected with mindfulness, as advocated by Somdech Preah Maha Ghosananda, Supreme Patriarch of Cambodia, and is rooted in the present moment, where there is no room for such negative emotions as hatred, anger, revenge, etc.[50] Similar insights are raised by the Vietnamese Buddhist master, Thich Nhat Hanh.[51] Another prominent Buddhist proponent of forgiveness is the Dalai Lama, at the heart of whose peace philosophy is the ability to cultivate forgiveness.[52]

Forgiveness in Buddhism is seen as a practice to prevent harmful thoughts from causing havoc on one's mental well-being.

145

Buddhism recognizes that feelings of hatred and ill will leave a lasting effect on our mind. Instead, Buddhism encourages the cultivation of thoughts that leave a wholesome effect. "If we haven't forgiven, we keep creating an identity around our pain, and that is what is reborn. That is what suffers."[53] One allegorical trajectory from Hinduism can lead to the nontheistic impulse in Buddhism and to a search for a way to live in a world of existential suffering, a reality affirmed in the first noble truth of Buddhism (*dukkha*), that the sufferings of this life become the basis for compassion, forbearance, and pity. Living in this way is to live in light of the perfections or moral qualities that have been cultivated to a maximal degree by Buddha, Buddhas, or the "awakened ones."[54] Against the broad variety of Buddhism, which generally divides into Theravada and Mahayana traditions (the Vajrayana tradition is often seen as a subset of Mahayana Buddhism)—both rejecting a creator God, or at least considering such to be irrelevant, while the latter holding to a role for a divine Buddha to guide humans to enlightenment, there is a notion of forgiveness lodged in the renunciation of anger or resentment toward someone who has offended you.

While the world may be a realm of suffering, it is not one of inherent injustice. Buddhists understand that justice is maintained by karma in which good actions are rewarded with good fruits and bad with bad fruits. In this sense there is a kind of metaphysics behind Buddhism, if not in as theistic or robust a fashion as with the Abrahamic traditions. This attitude toward understanding forgiveness in the context of wisdom, compassion, and forbearance lends a certain existential quality to Buddhist conceptions of forgiveness. Understood as such, this perspective has fostered the powerful contemporary movement of "engaged Buddhism," a movement characterized by "caring and service, social and environmental protest and analysis, and nonviolence as a creative way of overcoming conflict...."[55] The affirmation of life in the face of suffering, manifested in a "culture of awakening," or mindfulness, can lead to a more humane world, socially just and ecologically sustainable in the sense of a recognition, inherent to various

Theravada, Mahayana, and Vajrayana Buddhist traditions, that all beings suffer and that we share in the sufferings of others. In this sense, then, living with forgiveness is to live in an existential and compassionate fashion with all living beings.[56]

JAIN

While Buddhism evolved in the eastern part of India (ca. 563 BCE), another Hindu reform movement was also underway, although more ascetic and oriented to ritual, Jainism (in and around 550 BCE). It also exists into the modern era and, as with Buddhism, forgiveness finds a prominent place in the Jain community along with such virtues as love, joy, and peace. Similarly, forgiveness can only be achieved through caring for others, understanding the pain of others, and reaching out to other human beings. Forgiveness plays a prominent role in the Jain community, as it gives form to one of the two major annual Jain festivals, Paryushan, the other being Diwali, the commemoration of the nirvana of Lord Mahaviara, sage who established the essential tenets of Jainism.

Paryushan is the time when monks and nuns stay in community to foster spiritual instruction and guidance. Followed by both major Jain sects (Shvetambars and Digambars), this is a time of study, reflection, and purification, an opportunity for looking inward. For Shvetambars, the final day of Paryushan is Samvastsari Pratikraman, the "Annual Confession." This provides opportunity for confession and restoration. It involves a ritual of asking forgiveness from one's teacher, family, and friends and, finally, from all living beings. The culmination of confession is receiving forgiveness from all living beings and granting forgiveness to all beings. As the ritual has evolved in the United States, it is sometimes called the rite of "universal friendship."[57]

Aboriginal and Indigenous Belief and Practice

Aboriginal and indigenous religion forms a third broad approach to an understanding of how religious traditions frame conceptions of forgiveness. Most aboriginal and indigenous traditions are essentially tribal and animistic. They often share in a belief that ever-present spirits are at work in human beings and nature alike. There is often no sharp distinction between the sacred and secular, between the spirits and the essential unity of nature and humanity. In the case of personal and community infractions, there is often a preference for teaching and healing, and away from punishment. Forgiveness often functions in a communal sense, with an emphasis upon a kind of restorative justice that enables community restoration that is inclusive of both victim and offender.

NORTH AMERICAN INDIGENOUS RELIGION

An emphasis upon bringing offenders into a "healing circle" for purposes of community health is seen, for example, among the North American Cree and Ojibway First Nations. Forgiveness becomes framed by restoration to community. In many aboriginal or native cultures, a real harm in the case of individual or community infraction is seen to have been done to all. Working with many remote Oji-Cree community in northwestern Ontario, Rupert Ross, Assistant Crown attorney for the region writes of ways by which forgiveness fits into a pattern of holistic teaching and healing, rather than punishment.

This has been important among Tlingits for dealing with community offenders in which a judge agrees to a community request for a healing disposition, whereby working out the implications of forgiveness in the context of community living is seen to foster restorative justice. Ross writes, "A community disposition continues that humiliation, at least until full forgiveness has been achieved. A gaol sentence removes the offender from this daily accountability, may not do anything towards rehabilitation, and for many will actually be an easier disposition than staying in the community."[58]

This emphasis upon placing forgiveness in the context of community, and of community restoration, finds further support in the Navajo Tribal Court, recognized as a leading institution among tribal peoples.[59] According to Ross, one of the leading supporters of the move toward peacemaker courts, Chief Justice of the Navajo Nation Judicial Branch, Robert Yazzie, argues for the involvement of people who are a part of the dispute making the decisions. He finds an important role for Navajo wise persons, *naat'aanii*, or elders to provide guidance, encourage talk about the problems at hand, not to make decisions for others, but to foster decisions through guidance. Different from a western mediator or arbitrator, the role of the elders is to guide parties back into the thoughts and behaviors that reflect indigenous values.[60]

This emphasis upon community healing among aboriginal and indigenous groups is toward the restoration of social and individual health, but it also carries a deep source of shared meaning seen in a recent "discovery" by North American Mi'kmaq people. In an effort to restore their language to everyday use, it is said that they "found" an ancient verb tense that had fallen into disuse, a tense specifically designed to say to everyone: "This event has been concluded to the satisfaction of all." In English, they have called this the "Forgiveness Tense." It is a way of implying to the entire community that victims are healed, offenders restored, and the community able to put behind the infraction encountered.[61] It is an understanding that has helped to shape the contemporary restorative justice movement throughout the legal community.[62]

Australian and South Pacific Aboriginal Religion

In addition to an enveloping restorative justice, as we have noted in North American aboriginal and indigenous communities, justice and the role played by forgiveness find themselves embedded in a larger world of meaning that is communal in ways that include the living and their ancestors.[63] This is evident among other aboriginal peoples throughout the world and through the growing links of aboriginal and indigenous people in one area of the world with other indigenous peoples throughout the world.[64]

In Australian aboriginal religion, ancestors provide the model for life; establish a pattern for the daily round of economic, political, social, cultural, and ritual activities; and provide the traditions and experiences, stories, ceremonies, values, and structures that sustain a people.[65] Relationships are of vital importance and dictate much of the day-to-day behavior of individuals. These relationships and their obligations include the Ancestral Spirit Beings. The rules, taboos, and punishments that are enshrined in *The Dreaming* stories are the "legal" pattern for life, however disrupted by colonization and non-indigenous cultures.[66] Aboriginal songwriter, the late Kevin Gilbert, writes of the interpenetrating reality of creator and creation, a holistic integration that defines the aboriginal worldview. In her book, *The Search for Meaning*, the broadcaster Caroline Jones, has written that, "Aboriginal people gave meaning to my life by showing through their suffering, their courage, their unselfishness, their sense of family, their forgiveness, their survival and their sense of the sacred what it is truly like to be human."[67] Rituals, acts of forgiveness, are a part of the holistic integration of life, as there is no sharp distinction between the sacred and secular, between the spirits, nature, and humanity.

This integrative attitude is seen in Family Group Conferencing. Family Group Conferences (FGC), based on the teachings of the Maori (the aboriginal people of New Zealand) and used with all young offenders, are grounded in the four elements of pre-European Maori society: first, the importance of reaching consensus with the whole community; second, seeking as the desired outcome, reconciliation and a settlement acceptable to all parties; third, a concern not to apportion blame but to examine wider reasons for the wrong; and, finally, placing primary focus on the restoration of harmony. Again, as in North American indigenous communities, dealing with crime and locating the role of forgiveness within the community has been to foster healing, not punishment. Australian criminologists, John Braithwaite and Stephen Mugford, reviewing the FGC process in New Zealand and in the

Australian community of Wagga Wagga, have noted the capacity of FGCs to soften or prevent stigmatizing or degrading attacks on the offender as a person, instead placing shame on the act.[68] Forgiveness is seen to be related to community harmony and restorative justice.

As indigenous communities, such as, those in North America, Australia, or New Zealand, wrestle with the dilemmas of apology, forgiveness, and reconciliation, these restorative and communal dimensions of forgiveness must be kept in mind for there to be a sense of legitimacy for forgiveness sought and forgiveness granted. While the word is the same, different conceptions of forgiveness course through indigenous and non-indigenous communities. Apology for oppression and violence are perceived in different ways by different cultural and religious communities. Issues of language and perspective need to be negotiated, as much as any other aspect or consideration, for there to be practical reconciliation.[69]

African Indigenous

African indigenous religions participate in much of the same world view as indigenous and aboriginal religion throughout the world. The holistic aspect of this has been frequently raised up in connection with the term *ubuntu*, of Bantu origin but seen as a classical African concept and made prominent by Nelson Mandela and Desmond Tutu in the context of South Africa's struggle with Apartheid. The term focuses on a people's allegiances and relations with each other.[70]

In the effort to move toward forgiveness and what we might see as its logical end—reconciliation—there is the need for truth. The difficulty in clearly understanding the nature of truth is often seen in truth commissions and other public inquiries into the nature of truth. For example, through the procedures of the South Africa Truth and Reconciliation Commission, four forms of truth were identified: factual or forensic truth, personal or narrative truth, social or "dialogue" truth, and healing or restorative truth. Most truth commissions focus on factual or forensic truth that

151

seeks to ground itself in impartial or objective evidence. However, the recovery of truth often finds itself framed by processes that wrestle with personal narratives and dialogue in a journey that leads to the restoration of relationships.[71]

Such restoration or reconciliation requires truth. It cannot be manipulated. The effort to understand the truth of a given event, of a situation, or of a relationship does not come easily. The idea of *ubuntu* reminds us of the contextual nature of truth, that truth is always a part of a larger framework of community and of meaning, which needs to be incorporated into consciousness if the decision for forgiveness is to be made, the subsequent re-humanization of the other to happen, and justice to be found in the pursuit of reconciliation. Human beings and their societies are vulnerable to natural and cultural breakdown. Aboriginal and indigenous cultures remind us that this general instability touches all aspects of our lives, and that rituals of forgiveness, in the context of community, are means of restoration.[72]

In Conclusion

Research will continue on the nature of forgiveness, as to whether humanity is hardwired to forgive or whether forgiveness is a part of evolving culture. This research will take us to dialogue with the efficacy of religion, or of the wisdom traditions, in fostering forgiveness, which is to say, in fostering individual and communal health. This article has attempted to explore the trajectories of healing and forgiveness in the three families of religion noted here: Abrahamic, Indic, and Aboriginal. Each encompasses its own broad approach to an understanding of the nature and practice of forgiveness. The Abrahamic traditions are most clearly grounded in a theistic ontology and related to conceptions of justice and mercy. The Indic traditions affirm the existential value of forgiveness as an aspect of mindfulness and compassion. Aboriginal and indigenous religions draw our attention to issues of community and dignity through restorative justice. Each of these three broad ways of understanding forgiveness deserves further research for what it offers to the healing of persons and communities and to the repair of the world, so central to human identity that, in the words of Elizabeth Spelman, we might think of ourselves as *"homo reparans."*[73]

Notes

1. Sigmund Freud, "The Question of a Weltanschauung," in *New Introductory Lectures on Psychoanalysis*, trans. and ed. James Strachey (New York: W. W. Norton, 1964), 195–96.

2. Other competitors included Marxist philosophy, which found—in religion—an asymmetrical relation to life's real needs, Karl Marx and Friedrich Engels, *On Religion* (Mineola, NY: Dover Publications, 2008), 69ff.

3. Emile Durkheim, *Suicide*, ed. George Simpson, trans. John Spaulding (1897; New York: Free Press, 1997), 104, 297 passim.

4. Rudolf Otto, *The Idea of the Holy*, 2nd ed. (New York: Oxford University Press, 1958).

5. Scott R. Appleby, *The Ambivalence of the Sacred: Religion, Violence, and Reconciliation*, Carnegie Commission on Preventing Deadly Conflict (New York: Rowman & Littlefield Publishers, 1999).

6. Hannah Arendt, *The Human Condition:A Study of the Central Dilemmas Facing Modern Man* (Doubleday Anchor Books, 1959), 239, citing Luke 5:21–24, Matthew 9:4–6, and Mark 12:7–10. Arendt implies by this that humans, like God, can forgive in the sense of releasing each other from the consequences of the past. Forgiveness facilitates the emergence of new and unforeseen initiatives and "interrupts" how things might otherwise have been.

7. Mark Amstutz, *The Healing of Nations: The Promise and Limits of Political Forgiveness* (Lanham, MD: Rowman & Littlefield, 2005).

8. Leonel Narvaez Gomez, Foundation for Reconciliation, "Schools of Forgiveness and Reconciliation: Theory and Method" (BTI Seminar Workshop, Bogotá, Colombia, June 1–15, 2010). Violence affects the psyche of those who are challenged in the

basic pillars of their personality. For example, in the face of loss to a sense of personal safety, loss of confidence in social relationships, or challenges to one's sense of meaning, forgiveness stands as a means of healing and toward a restoration of meaning.

9. Lewis B. Smedes, *The Art of Forgiving* (Nashville, TN: Moorings, 1996). Three examples of contemporary research include: Robert Enright and the Human Development Study Group at the University of Madison, WI, have illustrated how forgiveness leads to improved physical and mental health and better relationships. See Enright, *Forgiveness Is a Choice: A Step-By-Step Process for Resolving Anger and Restoring Hope* (Washington, DC: American Psychological Association, 2001). Working out of the Department of Psychology at Virginia Commonwealth University, Everett Worthington has developed an evidence-based approach to illustrate the effectiveness of forgiveness and reconciliation. See his book, *Forgiveness and Reconciliation: Theory and Application* (New York: Brunner-Routledge, 2006). Michael McCullough, in *Beyond Revenge: The Evolution of the Forgiveness Instinct* (San Francisco, CA: Jossey-Bass, 2008), argues that despite popular belief that revenge is a disease, both revenge and forgiveness have been adaptive for our species. While acknowledging that cycles of revenge seem unbreakable, he sees evidence of humanity's collective will to break these cycles through innovative behavior, such as, restorative justice, truth, and reconciliation commissions, and humanity's hardwired impulse to forgive.

10. J. Cordova and others, "Behavior Analysis of Forgiveness in Couples Therapy" *International Journal of Behavioral Consultation and Therapy* 2, no. 2(2006): 192.

11. Dr. Robert Enright, *Forgiveness is a Choice* (Philadelphia: American Psychological Association, 2001).

12. J. Maltby and others, "Personality Predictors of Levels of Forgiveness Two and a Half Years After the Transgression," *Journal of Research in Personality* 42 (2008): 1088–94.

13. Everett L. Worthington Jr., *Dimensions of Forgiveness: Psychological Research and Theological Perspectives* (Philadelphia, PA: Templeton, 1998).

14. Robert D. Enright and Joanna North, eds., *Exploring Forgiveness* (University of Wisconsin, 1998), 20.

15. "Forgiving," Campaign for Forgiveness Research, http://www.forgiving.org (2006).

16. C. Van Oyen and others, "Granting Forgiveness or Harboring Grudges: Implications for Emotions, Physiology and Health," *Psychological Science* 12 (2001):117–23.

17. Sid Sarinopoulos, "Forgiveness and Physical Health: A Doctoral Dissertation Summary," *World of Forgiveness* 2 (2000): 16–18.

18. Andrew B. Newberg and others, "The Neurophysiological Correlates of Forgiveness," in *Forgiveness: Theory, Research, and Practice,* ed. Michael E. McCollough, Kenneth I. Pargament, and Carl E. Thoresen (New York: Guilford Press, 2001), 91–98.

19. Worthington, *Dimensions of Forgiveness,* 113–18.

20. *Forgive for Good: A Proven Prescription for Health and Happiness* (New York: HarperOne, 2003). See www.http://en.wikipedia.org/wiki/Forgiveness - cite_ref-8#cite_ref-8Learningto forgive.com.

21. Everett L. Worthington Jr., "The Pyramid Model of Forgiveness: Some Interdisciplinary Speculations about Unforgiveness and the Promotion of Forgiveness." in *Dimensions of Forgiveness: Psychological Research & Theological Perspectives.* ed. Everett L. Worthington Jr. (Philadelphia: Templeton Foundation Press, 1998), 129.

22. According to researcher Linda Radzik, atonement and reconciliation can be considered as two sides of the same coin, as far as they both imply the restoration of a relation that has been damaged. Radzik describes the result of wrongdoing as the diminishing of the value of the victim, which has personal and social implications. See her study, Linda Radzik, *Making Amends: Atonement in Morality, Law, and Politics* (Oxford: Oxford University Press, 2009), 76–78.

23. Michael E. McCullough, Kenneth I. Pargament, and Carl E. Thoresen, eds., *Forgiveness: Theory, Research, and Practice* (New York: The Guilford Press, 2001), 17–40.

24. McCullough, *Beyond Revenge,* 112–33.

25. Leonard Swidler, Khalid Duran, and Reuven Firestone, *Trialogue: Jews, Christians, and Muslims in Dialogue* (New London, CT: Twenty-Third Publications, 2007): 198–99.

26. JewFAQ discussion of forgiveness on Yom Kippur, http://jewfaq.org/holiday4.html

27. Jonathan Sacks, "Covenant and Conversation" http://www.chiefrabbi.org/2012/12/17/covenant-conversation-vayi gash-choice-and-change/ (accessed January 8, 2013).

28. Elliot N. Dorff, "Religious Perspectives on Forgiveness," in *Forgiveness: Theory, Research and Practice*, ed. Michael E. McCullough, Kenneth I. Pargament, and Carl E. Thoresen, 23–24 (New York: The Guilford Press, 2001).

29. Solomon Shimmel, *Wounds Not Healed by Time: The Power of Repentance and Forgiveness* (New York: Oxford University Press, 2004).

30. Simon Wiesenthal, *The Sunflower* (New York: Shocken Books, 1976).

31. Louis E. Newman, "The Quality of Mercy: On the Duty to Forgive in the Judaic Tradition," *Journal of Religious Ethics* 15 (1987): 155–72; cf. Elliot N. Dorff, "The Elements of Forgiveness: A Jewish Approach," in *Dimensions of Forgiveness*, ed. Everett L. Worthington (Philadelphia: John Templeton Press, 1998), 29–55.

32. James G. Williams, "Religious Perspectives on Forgiveness," in *Forgiveness: Theory, Research and Practice*, ed. Michael E. McCullough, Kenneth I. Pargament, and Carl E. Thoresen, 24–25 (New York: The Guilford Press, 2001).

33. Gustaf Aulen, *Christus Victor: An Historical Study of the Three Main Types of the Idea of Atonement* (Wipf & Stock Publishers, 2003). See Mark Heim, *Saved From Sacrifice: A Theology of the Cross* (Grand Rapids: Eerdmans, 2006).

34. Alexander Roberts and James Donaldson, eds., *Apostolic Constitutions: The Ante-Nicene Fathers* (Buffalo, NY: The Christian Literature Co., 1886), 7:402.

35. Modern English Translation of the *Holy Qur'an*. From the original work of A. Yusuf Ali (Kansas City, MO: Manar Int'l Corp., 1998).

36. Dr. Muzzamil Siddiqi, "Forgiveness: Islamic Persepctive," Islam Online, August 6, 2004, http://www.islamonline.com/news/articles/6/Forgiveness_Islamic_Perspective.html (accessed February 7, 2009).

37. "Forgiveness in Islam," Summary of a Friday Khutbah, April 14, 2000, http://www.islamawareness.net/Salvation/forgive ness.html (accessed January 7, 2013).

38. Chawkat Moucarry, *The Search for Forgiveness: Pardon and Punishment in Islam and Christianity* (Leicester, England: InterVarsity Press, 2004). Moucarry explores the Islamic understanding of forgiveness, finding it in tension with competing claims of justice and mercy in the attributes of Allah.

39. M. Amir Ali, "Religious Perspectives on Forgiveness," in *Forgiveness: Theory, Research and Practice*, ed. Michael E. McCullough, Kenneth I. Pargament, and Carl E. Thoresen, 25–27 (New York: The Guilford Press, 2001).

40. Moucarry, *The Search for Forgiveness*, 150.

41. It is important to see the Islamic renewal in the context of global, not merely, European history. See Samir Amin, *Eurocentrism*, trans. Russell Moore (New York: Monthly Review Press, 1989).

42. Mark Juergensmeyer, *Terror in the Mind of God: The Global Rise of Religious Violence* (Berkeley: University of California Press, 2000).

43. Evelin Lindner, *Making Enemies: Humiliation and International Conflict* (Westport, CT: Praeger Security International, 2006).

44. Qaiser Shahzad, "Ibn 'Arabi's Contribution to the Ethics of Divine Names," *Islamic Studies*, 43, no. 1 (Spring 2004): 5–38.

45. As in Beck, "Religious Perspectives on Forgiveness," *Forgiveness: Theory, Research and Practice*, ed. Michael E. McCullough, Kenneth I. Pargament, and Carl E. Thoresen, 29–30 (New York: The Guilford Press, 2001).

46. Rajmohan Gandhi, "The Righteous Chariot," in *No Enemy to Conquer: Forgiveness in an Unforgiving World*, ed. Michael Henderson (Waco: Baylor University Press, 2009), 106–8.

47. I am following Beck, in "Religious Perspectives on Forgiveness," in *Forgiveness: Theory, Research and Practice*, ed. Michael E. McCullough, Kenneth I. Pargament, and Carl E. Thoresen, 107 (New York: The Guilford Press, 2001).

48. Gandhi in Henderson, *No Enemy to Conquer*, 107.

49. "Triumph of the Spirit," in *The Future of Peace: On the Front Lines with the World's Great Peacemakers*, ed. Scott A. Hunt (New York: HarperOne, 2004), 40.

50. Maha Ghosananda, *Step by Step* (Parallax Press, 1991).

51. Thich Nhat Hanh, *Taming the Tiger Within: Meditations on Transforming Difficult Emotions* (New York: Riverhead Trade, 2005).

52. His Holiness the Dalai Lama and Victor Chan, *The Wisdom of Forgiveness: Intimate Conversations and Journeys* (New York: Riverhead Books, 2004), 46.

53. "Yamakavagga: Pairs," translated from Pali by Thanissaro Bhhikkhu (1997–2013) Accesstoinsight.org (accessed January 7, 2013).

54. Hallisey, "Religious Perspectives on Forgiveness," in *Forgiveness: Theory, Research and Practice*, ed. Michael E. McCullough, Kenneth I. Pargament, and Carl E. Thoresen, 27–29 (New York: The Guilford Press, 2001).

55. Ken Jones and Kenneth Kraft, *The New Social Face of Buddhism: A Call to Action* (Wisdom Publications, 2003).

56. David Chappell, *Buddhist Peacework: Creating Cultures of Peace* (Somerville, MA: Wisdom Publications, 2000).

57. Bharat S. Shah, *An Introduction to Jainism* (New York: Setubandh Publications, 2002). See in, *On Common Ground: World Religions in America* (five CD-ROM Multipack Set) by Diana L. Eck and Pluralism Project at Harvard University (New York: Columbia University Press, 2002).

58. Rupert Ross, *Returning to the Teachings: Exploring Aboriginal Justice* (Toronto: Penguin Canada, 1996), 17–18.

59. See Philmer Bluehouse, coordinator of the Navajo Peacemaker Court, and James Zion, solicitor to the Courts of the Navajo nation, in "The Navajo Justice and Peace Ceremony," *The Mediation Quarterly* (1982); cited in Ross, *Returning to the Teachings*, 25–26.

60. Another example of the context of community comes from the province of Manitoba, and the Ojibway community of Hollow Water. The Community Holistic Circle Healing Program at Hollow Water offers an illustration of the way by which a healing strategy envelops the concept for forgiveness and leads, not

just to the restoration of social and individual health in aboriginal community, but also to deeper sources of meaning, identity, purpose, and fulfillment in life. This is exemplified in the principles shared by Ojibway and Mi'kmaq peoples found in the book, *The Sacred Tree*, produced by over thirty elders, spiritual teachers, and professionals from aboriginal communities across North America. *The Sacred Tree* (Four Worlds Development Press, Four World's Development Project, University of Lethbridge, 4401 University Drive, Lethbridge, Alberta, Canada T1K 3M4, 1984).

61. Ross, *Returning to the Teachings*, 188–89.

62. Michael L. Hadley, ed., *The Spiritual Roots of Restorative Justice* (Albany: State University of New York, 2001).

63. Bill Edwards, "Living the Dreaming," in *Aboriginal Australia*, ed. Colin Bourke, Eleanor Bourke, and Bill Edwards, 77–99 (University of Queensland Press, 1998).

64. See meeting of aboriginal delegates with other indigenous peoples in New Zealand at the World Conference on Spiritual Healing (1993) in *Aboriginal Australia*, ed. Colin Bourke, Eleanor Bourke, and Bill Edwards, 96 (University of Queensland Press, 1998).

65. Djiniyini Gondarra, *Father You Gave Us the Dreaming* (Darwin: Bethel Presbytery, 1988).

66. Edwards, "Living the Dreaming," 85.

67. Caroline Jones, *The Search for Meaning* (Crows Nest, NSW: Australian Broadcasting Company, 1989), 17.

68. In 1989, the government of New Zealand passed the Children, Young Persons and Their Families Act, creating the new process called the Family Group Conference (FGC), extending it to youth charged with criminal offenses other than the most serious cases, the condition being that offenders accept responsibility for what they have been charged. See Ross, *Returning to the Teachings*, 19.

69. David Mellor, Di Bretherton, and Lucy Firth, "Aboriginal and Non-aboriginal Australia: The Dilemma of Apologies, Forgiveness, and Reconciliation," *Peace and Conflict: Journal of Peace Psychology*, vol. 13, no. 1 (2007): 11–36.

70. Desmond Tutu, *No Future Without Forgiveness* (New York: Image, 2000); see D. M. Swanson, "Ubuntu: An African

Contribution to (Re)search for/with a 'Humble Togetherness,' " *The Journal of Contemporary Issues in Education*, 2, no.2, University of Alberta, Special Edition on African Worldviews (2007).

71. Hugo Van der Merwe and Audrey Chapman, *Truth and Reconciliation in South Africa: Did the TRC Deliver?* (University of Pennsylvania, 2008), 244.

72. Malidoma Patrice Some, *The Healing Wisdom of Africa* (New York: Tarcher/Putnam, 1998).

73. Elizabeth V. Spelman, *Repair; The Impulse to Restore in a Fragile World* (Boston: Beacon Press, 2002), 85–87. Spelman bases her thesis on the argument that the human being is a repairing animal. Forgiveness is the means of repair.

V
PASTORAL
APPROACHES

10

THE PRACTICE OF FORGIVENESS

Frank Desiderio, CSP

Have you ever felt eaten up by resentment? You know, when someone insults you and you can't stop thinking about it? You keep refining the cutting comebacks you wish you'd said. Or maybe you've suffered some deep betrayal, when someone you loved lied to you or left you. Over and over in the shower, in the car, in the middle of the night, you revisit and replay it in your mind. Then one day, you share your sad, sad story with a well-meaning friend, who says, "Oh, why don't you just let it go!" And you say, "Let it go? I'd love to. But how do I do that?"

How to let go is the skill I teach in *Letting Go of a Grudge* retreats, workshops, and parish missions. Yes, forgiveness is a skill, and you can learn it. People wrestling with resentment come to learn how to slip out of the grip of the past, release their emotional burden, and move forward with some peace. They come to take advantage of this opportunity to actually release the resentment or hurt feelings or revenge thoughts they've been holding onto and get some freedom.

The retreat is where their own willingness and God's grace come together to bring healing. And it works. Over and over again, during the exercises, presentations, meditations, and prayer services, I see the door opening for grace to work in the lives of participants. I see the transformation when people let go of the anger or sadness they've been carrying in the wake of a long-standing hurt. I see the healing happen when they forgive others for some fraud or infidelity, forgive themselves for some mistake they've made, forgive God for some tragedy or violent twist in their lives. They let go of their burden, so it can be lifted from them.

Letting Go of a Grudge helps participants understand and put into practice the spirituality of forgiveness. They learn the five-step process for letting go of a grudge and, if it's the right thing to do, reconciling with the person or institution that hurt them.

The Theology of Letting Go of a Grudge

"Then God said, 'Let us make humankind in our image, according to our likeness…'" (Gen 1:26a).

In the first chapter of the Bible, we're told that we're made in the image and likeness of God. Toward the end of the Bible, having seen the evidence of Jesus' life, we're told what that means exactly, "*so we have known and believe the love that God has for us. God is love, and those who abide in love abide in God, and God abides in them*" (1 John 4:16).

God is love, and we are made in the image of God. That means we are created to love. The big question is this: Can we love the way God loves?

Sometimes love is easy. When we see a baby, especially our own, we can't help but love. When we meet the girl or boy of our dreams and fall in love, love is easy. But what about when that child grows up and rejects us? What about when the dream relationship turns into a nightmare? When love is hard, how can we love? God gave us Jesus Christ to show us how to love, even when it's hard, even in the shadow of the cross. We are created in God's image, so we are created to be like Jesus—that is, to empty ourselves of all that is not love (Phil 2:6–7a).

Forgiveness is a primary way for us to become what we are made to be, because it requires us to empty ourselves of our anger and hurt so we can give the gift of forgiveness to another. "*But I say to you, Love your enemies and pray for those who persecute you, so that you may be children of your Father in heaven"* (Matt 5:44–45a). We may not be able to love on our own, but we can let Christ love our "enemies" through us.

It was the poet, Alexander Pope, who said, *"To err is human, to forgive divine."* It's human to make mistakes, to damage our relationships. On our own as humans, we can't fully forgive. The beginning of real forgiveness is a gift, a grace—that is, the gift of God's Spirit working in us. God forgives us and gives us the grace to forgive others. When we forgive, we are participating in the divine.

Christians are disciples of Christ. That means they follow the discipline offered by Christ to his followers, and forgiveness is a part of that discipline. As we practice forgiveness, we get better at it. I've learned this in my own life: in order to be a forgiving person, I have to forgive. The more I do it, the better I am at it, so I keep practicing.

Prior to the Practice of Forgiveness

In the *Letting Go of a Grudge* parish mission, before getting into the actual practice of forgiveness, we examine basic themes that trip people up on the way to forgiveness:

- What forgiveness is and what it is not.
- What is the relationship between justice and forgiveness?
- How do we deal with anger and revenge?
- Are some things unforgivable?

A key to our understanding is that there are two types of forgiveness: conditional forgiveness and unconditional forgiveness.

Conditional Forgiveness

Conditional forgiveness means some condition must be met before the offended person will grant forgiveness. Usually that condition is an apology from the offender. The offended person may want the culprit to show remorse and express regret—or sometimes make some compensation for the damage. In order to satisfy the offended person's demands for justice, forgiveness isn't given until such conditions are met.

Unconditional Forgiveness

Unconditional forgiveness is letting go of negative feelings. Perhaps there is no apology forthcoming. Perhaps the offending person has died or disappeared. For whatever reason, it may now be impossible to ever get the justice that comes from an apology or restitution. But even if conditional forgiveness isn't possible, we can still make a choice to "let go." Even if the hurt party may still wish the perpetrator brought to justice, she or he can make a decision to not continue to hold hatred or hurt in her or his heart.

This sort of release of negative feelings is what I call "letting go." It is possible to want justice, but to not seek revenge and retaliation anyway. It is possible to want what is right, but not hold onto the hurt. As I say on the retreat, "It's okay to seek justice, but do you hire a lawyer or a hit man?"

The Program for Letting Go of a Grudge

The process of LETTING GO is designed to teach people how make forgiveness a way of life.

I suggest you start learning about forgiveness with a small- to moderate-sized resentment. Think of a random resentment that you have. It could be current or in the past. Not a giant one. Not the parent who abandoned you, not the spouse who divorced you, not the murderer who killed your loved one, not the lover who broke your heart, not the person who sexually abused you. Those are enormous hurts. You want to work your way up to forgiving big hurts by starting with a small- to medium-sized hurt. Something that still grates at you—like not being invited to a wedding or the girl who said, "I'm just not that into you" or the boss who didn't give you the bonus you deserved. I suggest people use this kind of resentment in the exercises we do.

After individuals become masters of forgiveness, that's when they can take on the heroic job of forgiving what we can call "the unforgivable." Now it's true that, for the Christian, nothing is unforgivable because nothing is unredeemable. In the power of Christ's resurrection, we can bring new life out of death. But just as there was a day between Good Friday and Easter Sunday, in this instance we may have to live in Holy Saturday for a time— because with forgiveness, timing is crucial.

While doing a parish mission in a Midwestern state, I met a woman who told me a story. Her daughter, a young teacher at the time, was hit by a drunk driver. It took five surgeries and a long time to put her broken body back together. As she lay in her hospital bed, just two days after the accident, even before the physical healing started, a Eucharistic minister from the local parish visited her. After listening to her, the poorly trained minister said, "I won't give you communion until you forgive the man who did this to you."

The young woman was in no mood to forgive. Over and beyond the pain and fear for her physical health, she was still feeling the shock and outrage at what had been done to her. So not only did she not get communion, she wrote off the Church and was finished with God. It was only much, much later that a caring priest undid the damage, and she was able to move on with her life. She came to accept what the drunk driver did to her. She also forgave the poor minister and is now back as a member of the Church.

Back in those first confusing, painful, emotional days after the accident, there was no time, no room, no place for forgiveness. It would have been better for the minister to have acknowledged the woman's anger at the inflictor of such injury on her and assured her of God's presence, even in the terrible situation she was in. After a tragedy, we have to recognize the enormity of what has happened, go through a period of outrage, mourn our losses, and honor our grief. If someone has just gone through a terrible hurt—the murder of a child, betrayal by a spouse, their house burned down by a careless neighbor—to suggest immediately that they forgive is unreasonable, even silly. After they have experienced the normal course of strong emotions brought on by horrific heartbreaks and are tired of feeling terrible, then there may come a day when they realize they're worn out from being twisted through the wringer of these intense emotions, and they will want to stretch their spirits in the sun and move on. That is the day when they can start the process of forgiveness. It is, then, that they're ready to begin seeking the grace of letting go.

Forgiveness is a process. There is no magic. There is only the spiritual work and the grace of God helping us through to the "new normal." How do we get there?

The Five Steps of Letting Go of a Grudge

The heart of the *Letting Go of a Grudge* parish mission is practicing the five steps of forgiveness.[1] As we go through each step, I offer scriptural reflections, breathing meditation practice, and written exercises.

The five steps to *Letting Go of a Grudge* are:

- Look deeply at what went wrong.
- Empathy is the key.
- *Tell the story differently.*
- Give forgiveness freely.
- One day at a time, keep forgiveness strong.

STEP ONE—LOOK DEEPLY AT WHAT WENT WRONG

The beginning of forgiveness is honesty—an honest and clear-eyed look at the reality of what happened. We drill down deep and ask ourselves, "What *really* happened?" Not just the facts, but the feelings and the histories of the people involved. We want to get inside what happened and why. The point is to be really objective about the situation for the first time—to get out of the blame game and the litany of self-justification and into awareness of the cold hard reality of what happened. A good place to start our deep look at what went wrong is to tell the story to another person, a supportive and objective person who can help us see the situation through another pair of eyes. Our purpose is not to elicit sympathy yet again, but to get at the truth.

We do this because we can't do this forgiveness work alone. On our own, we hold onto resentments forever. We need a community to heal. We have to be willing to ask others to help us. The person who listens and reflects back could be a religious professional, a professional counselor, or a discrete friend. The point is, it's good to have another person who's detached from the incident go over it and help you see:

- What do you think happened?
- What *really* happened?
- What did the other person do?
- What was your part?

I also suggest the participants write out the story of what happened, as if they were a disinterested newspaper reporter. Tell the story like a journalist would, from a third- person observer's point of view.

This first step helps construct a box around the incident. It reduces it to its proper size, just so big and no bigger, neither minimized nor exaggerated in importance within the context of our entire lives. The fact is, this incident is not the story of our entire lives. It doesn't have to take over all of our thinking and feeling. It doesn't have to take up more room in our lives then necessary anymore. It doesn't have to define us.

Now that we know what we are dealing with, we can move onto step two.

STEP TWO—EMPATHY FOR THE OTHER IS THE KEY

Before there can be forgiveness, there must be a human connection with the offender. We come to see the person who hurt us not as "the enemy" but as someone like ourselves. We want to see if we can connect with some feeling or fact of his life that can give us insight into who this person is and why she or he may have done the malefaction. We try to see the situation from the other person's point of view.

Empathy is a big concept that covers a whole range of responses:

- Pity: "Oh, that poor *thing.*"
- Understanding: "I think I understand."
- Sympathy: "Oh, that poor *person.*"
- Compassion: "I feel for that person and want to help."

The most basic level of empathy is to at least have pity on another person: "I feel sorry for him, and glad I'm not him." On the other end of the scale from this most basic form of human connection is loving kindness or charity, which is feeling what another is feeling and wanting the best for that person, being willing to act in a way that shows we carry his best interests in our heart.

On the retreats, we do exercises to cultivate empathy, to encourage us to stand on the common ground of our shared humanity with those we consider our offenders. For believers, prayer can be a gateway to empathy when we're having a hard time feeling any. We can pray for the gift of empathy, for understanding and compassion for the other person. We can find that the common ground of our humanity with another comes from our coming from the same Creator. We read in the first letter of Peter. *"Finally, all of you, have unity of spirit, sympathy, love for one another, a tender heart, and a humble mind. Do not repay evil for evil or abuse for abuse; but, on the contrary, repay with a blessing. It is for this that you were called—that you might inherit a blessing"* (1 Pet 3:8–9).

Once we have a good grasp on what happened and have some sense of empathy for the other person, then we're ready to move on to the next step.

Step Three—Tell the Story Differently

Often, when we tell our story, it's a victim's story: "This is what that so-and-so did to me." We rehash the particulars and live through the hurt again, re-traumatizing ourselves. If we want to forgive, we have to reframe our story.

Here's another way to tell it: "This is what that so-and-so did to me and it hurt, but *I've let go of my hard feelings for him.*" This reframes our story from tragedy to triumph. We have triumphed over the hurt we feel and moved on with our lives.

Another way to tell the story differently is to invite God into the story. In meditation, we invite a divine healer in. For some people, this will be Jesus, for others, it might be the Holy Spirit, and for others, it might be a saint such as the Blessed Virgin Mary. Invite this powerful, peaceful, healing presence into your meditation and ask for God to be present in the story and show how the story can have a different ending. How does God see it? Tell it from God's point of view. That will lead us to the next step.

Step Four—Give Forgiveness Freely

The fourth step in letting go is granting forgiveness. We give forgiveness as a gift. The person who hurt us may not deserve our forgiveness, which is why it's a gift.

The first thing to know is that we *decide* to forgive. We don't have to *feel* forgiving in order to forgive. Forgiveness is a conscious act. We can decide of our own free will to forgive. We can't control or change what the other person had done to us, but we can control or change our reaction to it. What forgiveness means is to *renounce revenge and release the person from any emotional debt we feel they owe us.*

On the retreat, we make a distinction between decisional forgiveness and emotional forgiveness. You can *decide* right now to forgive the person who hurt you, but it may take much longer to *feel* forgiveness in your heart. We talk about moving from decisional forgiveness to emotional forgiveness. One of the key ways to make this move is to pray for the other person.

Praying for the other person is our most powerful tool in the work of forgiveness. There is a dual benefit in it. For those who believe in the power of prayer, we ask God to bless the offender. We ask God to be present to them, and we extend our love to them magnified through God's all-powerful love. The second benefit of praying for the person is that it becomes harder and harder for us to hold hard feelings. When we pray for the other person, our heart softens, and we open ourselves up to empathy with him. While we're focusing on and practicing love and empathy, there is no resentment. Where there is no resentment, there is forgiveness.

STEP FIVE—ONE DAY AT A TIME, KEEP FORGIVENESS STRONG

As our hurts fade into memories, we wonder why we ever let them have so much power over us. We come to see new offenses more often as lessons, instead of transgressions. But some bigger or old, traumatic hurts may need to be dealt with again and again. When something horrific has happened to us in the past, we may forgive, but sometimes the searing pain will resurface. When it does, we have to be able to renew our decision to forgive. Each day, we have to be willing to apply the medicine of forgiveness to the pain of hurt and loss, no matter how big or small, no matter how many times.

Forgiveness also becomes a daily decision in the face of ongoing irritants, such as, a coworker who rubs us the wrong way or the annoying habits of a spouse. In life, conflict is inevitable. We're always going to bump up against the needs, reactions, and feelings of other people. When we encounter ordinary conflict, we need to address it. Some small things may be like snow and eventually melt away. But most conflicts are not healed by just ignoring them. Sometimes we might need to have a conversation with the person, so we can work toward what is best for all concerned—which is another way of saying "doing God's will."

When we've tried to resolve the conflict and are still left with a feeling of resentment, then there's one sure way to bridge what we see as an injustice gap, and that way is forgiveness. We have to be willing to forgive others to keep our relationships intact. Conflict happens. Forgive and move on. And if the old feelings of regret, revenge, retaliation, recrimination, and resentment rear their ugly heads again, we forgive and move on yet again.

Forgiveness Is a Way of Life

We have to be willing to be in the process of forgiveness daily. We want to take part in the ongoing journey that helps us become more spiritual, and forgiveness is the path. Each day, we take another step on that path. Through practice, we develop the discipline of running up and down the Five Steps of Forgiveness. As we persevere with the discipline, our practice deepens. We come to a more profound understanding of who we are and who we can be and who God is for us. We recognize our own false self, our shadow side, so we can call it out and not be controlled by our darker thoughts. And with practice, when we notice ourselves straying back into the shadows, we can gently and firmly move ourselves back onto the path.

Even in the midst of great upheaval or personal tragedies, we learn to live in the light, to find the serenity and deep joy that is our heritage. We learn to experience the healing of the spirit that comes from forgiveness.

Notes

1. My own model of how to forgive is directly indebted to the step-by-step process of forgiveness developed by Dr. Everett Worthington, Jr. of Virginia Commonwealth University.

11

COMPASSIONATE LISTENING: HEALING SKILLS AND SENSITIVITIES

Melissa M. Kelley

Introduction

At dinner recently, my toddler son began pointing toward the window and energetically proclaimed, "Plane! Plane!" For a moment, I was puzzled because, amid the background hum of our household, I did not hear a plane. But as I paused and listened carefully, I realized that he was right. There was a plane flying close by. My son, who has newly discovered the wonder of things that move in the sky, had brought a different sort of listening to the moment, and he heard what I almost missed.

We know well that careful listening is a critical cornerstone of all pastoral ministries. No one escapes a pastoral care course in seminary or ministry training without learning of the imperative to listen attentively to the other. However, I think our discussions of pastoral listening are sometimes incomplete. I would like to suggest four dimensions of pastoral listening that might need further clarification for us. First, what is the *essence* or defining feature of pastoral listening; that is, what is at its very heart? Second, what is the goal of pastoral listening, beyond the nebulous objective of helping others to feel that they have been "heard"? Pastoral ministers need a clear articulation of *why* they are listening—that is, the purpose and aim of pastoral listening. Third, given the fullness and complexity of many pastoral conversations, *what*, specifically, is it that ministers want to listen for as they attend to the other? And fourth, *how* can ministers best do pastoral listening; or in other words, what is required of the pastoral minister in order to be able to listen well to others? Although I am using the language of "pastoral minister" or "minister" in articulating and addressing these questions, I mean these terms in a broad sense to include all those who, on behalf of their communities of faith, try to offer a pastoral presence to others through careful and sensitive listening. Also, while I am largely addressing one-on-one listening by pastoral ministers, I believe that much of what I offer here applies to pastoral listening in group or communal settings as well.

The Essence of Pastoral Listening

Our first point for consideration is how we might describe the very heart or essence of pastoral listening. I would propose that *compassion* is at the core of all listening that aims to be pastoral. In its essence, pastoral listening is compassionate listening. As we know, the word *compassion*, in its Latin origins, means *to bear or suffer with or together*.[1] All of us know suffering of one sort or another. Some of us know profound suffering. This is one of the true universals of humanity. There is always someone on "humanity's mourning bench,"[2] as retired Yale theology professor Nicholas Wolterstorff has said. When we have compassion, we are in touch with this universal. We understand that, just as we suffer, so too do others suffer. Our suffering connects and unites us in our basic humanity, and thus, a part of us suffers with another who suffers. As Paul reminds us in First Corinthians, "If one member suffers, all suffer together with it" (1 Cor 12:26).[3]

And in our *suffering-with*, we feel moved to respond, to reach out to the other with kindness and care. This experience of feeling moved to respond may sometimes occur quite literally. I remember a friend describing an incident in which she was a passenger in a car traveling on a highway when she saw a person in distress by the side of the road. Although she was unable to stop the car, she felt her body—virtually on its own—begin to move sideways toward the person, so eager was she to respond to the person's need. This was a moment of true compassion. This sort of compassion marks pastoral listening to others. The pastoral minister listens carefully, is aware of the possible suffering of the other, and is moved to respond.

Of course, pastoral ministers have no monopoly on compassionate listening; various sorts of listening might best be described as compassionate. For example, many psychotherapists, whatever their particular therapeutic approach, describe the centrality of compassionate listening for their work. Yet from a Christian theological perspective, compassion is the very hallmark of pastoral listening, because Jesus Christ, our ultimate model for ministry, embodied compassion in his care of others. Again and again in the Christian Scriptures, we see Jesus deeply moved by the suffering of others.[4] Jesus, fully human and fully divine, knew well the experience of suffering—both his own and that of others, and he reached out to bring relief to the suffering he encountered. A deeply stirring example of this is his response in the Gospel of Luke to one of the two criminals crucified alongside him. As Jesus experienced his own agony on the cross, he listened to the suffering man's words and his plea that Jesus not forget him after death. Jesus was moved to respond; he promised that the man would be with him in paradise that very day (Luke 23:39–43). We might consider this a most touching ministerial moment, marked by careful listening and pure compassion. Author Susan Hedahl, writing for pastoral ministers, proposes that "listening is an act of patient friendship, love, and the very imaging of a listening God in our relationships."[5] That is, ministers represent our Listening God, who listens with compassion and responds with care, as Jesus did on the Cross. This is why compassion is the very hallmark of pastoral listening.

The Goal of Pastoral Listening

Our second point for consideration is the purpose or goal of pastoral listening. In other words, why is it important for pastoral ministers to listen compassionately to others? While it is risky to try to capture the goal of such a broad activity in a word or phrase, I would propose that a critical dimension of this goal is *healing*; that is, by listening compassionately to others, ministers hope to bring some healing to their suffering.

Healing is a rather nebulous term. What, precisely, does it mean? Many definitions of healing center on the idea of restoration of a person to health or wholeness, including "spiritual wholeness,"[6] and I find that this concept is apt in relation to pastoral listening. We can think of wholeness as one's sense of completeness, integrity, or well-being, with regard to oneself and one's world. Wholeness may also describe one's sense of completeness, integrity, or well-being in one's spiritual life, such as one's sense of connection to God and to humanity. This sense of wholeness may be threatened or even compromised at a time of suffering; that is, suffering or struggle may create some sort of pain or disruption to one's sense of completeness, well-being, and integrity in all aspects of one's life, including one's spiritual life. A person in this painful state often cries out for care and compassion, seeking help in returning to a sense of wholeness. At such moments, compassionate pastoral listening is a response to this cry, offering care that might help to restore the other's sense of wholeness; in so doing, compassionate listening helps to bring healing to the other.

In many professional worlds—such as clinical psychology and academia—we are currently in an era of "evidence-based practice"; this means that professionals are being asked to demonstrate or quantify that, in actuality, they do what they claim to do and their efforts are largely successful. For example, psychotherapists must often formulate treatment plans with clients that specify the goals of therapy as well as the measurable outcomes that will indicate that the goals have been met and the treatment has succeeded. While such expectations can sometimes have unwelcome effects—such as restricting creativity or spontaneity in one's process because of overly rigid structures of assessment—it is by and large both important and fair to ask for honest and searching appraisals of many professional endeavors, particularly when the well-being of others is at stake.

So, too, it is both fair and important for pastoral ministers to ask, what is the evidence that our actions have the desired effects? In other words, how do ministers know that their compassionate listening facilitates healing? Later in this essay, I will say more on the "evidence" of healing, after we consider some of the specifics of how compassionate pastoral listening may be practiced. For now, let us consider the idea that compassionate listening by pastoral ministers offers the potential for a critically needed sort of healing.

The Focus of Pastoral Listening

Our third point addresses a critical aspect of pastoral listening: for *what*, specifically, do ministers want to listen as they attend to others? With the barrage of noise that seems constantly to surround us, it can be a struggle—as it was for me at a busy dinner hour—to focus our listening so that we hear clearly and discriminately. I propose that pastoral listening demands particular sensitivities on the part of ministers in order to bring focus to their listening. In this section, I will present five such sensitivities that, I believe, are critically needed by pastoral ministers to listen in focused ways that facilitate healing.

First Sensitivity

Before I propose the first sensitivity for compassionate pastoral listening, we must spend a moment thinking about *story*. All of us tend to think of ourselves and our lives in terms of story or narrative. This is fundamental to who we are as humans. Human life, across time and across cultures, is grounded in significant ways in story or narrative.[7] When we think about our lives, we tend to arrange and consider the details and elements of our lives in story form. For instance, we consider the events and details of our lives *chronologically*, with a certain progression from beginning to middle to end. When we describe our lives, we highlight major and minor *characters*, and maybe both protagonists and antagonists. Our lives are often shaped by *themes*, those key ideas that form the central defining features or motivations of our lives, such as "family loyalty" or "For God and country." These are all examples of how fundamental *story* or *narrative* is in terms of how we understand our lives.

Our life story is both received and created. Each of us "inherits" significant parts of our story; we begin to learn about who we are and how we fit in our family and our world from our earliest days, through the storytelling of our significant caregivers, and through what we observe and learn growing up. But at some point in our lives, we typically also take a more active role in shaping or creating our own story; for instance, we decide what we want to pursue in terms of careers or relationships, and we begin to make decisions and choices to enact these parts of our story. Over time, our story reflects how we have come to understand the world and our place in it; it reflects our sense of completeness and integrity in life. Thus, our story articulates our sense of wholeness, as we considered wholeness above.

As we begin to get to know others, we typically share some aspects of our story. And as we know, people often share the story of their lives in great detail with their pastoral ministers. Therefore, the first sensitivity for compassionate pastoral listening is to *listen for the story*. That is, when listening pastorally to another, one wants to listen for the story elements that suggest how this person has organized the story of his or her life—past, present, and future— and how this person has constructed his or her sense of wholeness. One wants to listen for the narrative themes that help elucidate how this person understands self, life, and God.

179

As one listens for another's story, one will be coming to know the other in highly significant and personal ways; therefore, when listening for another's story, the minister is on truly sacred ground. This sort of listening is a sacred trust. As Mary Pellauer has said, "I have a very deep sense that there is nothing more beautiful than listening to people tell their stories about faith and God. They express, as nothing else can, who we really are and what we really believe in, and the meaning in our lives....If there's anything worth calling theology, it is listening to people's stories—listening to them and honoring and cherishing them."[8]

Second Sensitivity

As we know, what so often prompts people to speak with a pastoral minister is some sort of crisis or loss, and this brings us to the second sensitivity for pastoral listening, which is to *listen for the loss*. Above, we considered healing as having to do with restoration to wholeness. What is it that disrupts or shakes our sense of wholeness, thus prompting the need for healing? Such disruptions to our wholeness are often rooted in loss, the threat of loss, or the fear of loss. Therefore, in engaging with one who is suffering, the minister must listen for the sort(s) of loss that may be a significant part of the other's story.

It is possible that the sort of loss we are most familiar with is the loss of another through death. Of course, for many, the death of a loved one constitutes a tremendous loss and challenge for healing. But it is critical that we acknowledge that loss may occur in many forms other than or along with the death of another. Pastoral writers Kenneth Mitchell and Herbert Anderson have helpfully provided language for other sorts of loss that may challenge our sense of wholeness and prompt the need for healing.[9] For instance, a person who has been laid off from work may experience *role* loss (the loss of a familiar and important position or role); while a person who must surrender a cherished dream because of injury or aging, may experience *intrapsychic* loss (a loss within one's own psyche or to one's sense of self, such as abandoning some of one's expectations for the future). Sometimes we may be unaware that we have experienced a significant loss, but the effects of the loss may challenge us nonetheless, shaking or even decimating our story and our sense of wholeness embedded therein. For instance, aging often brings with it many losses, such as, deterioration of eyesight or forced retirement from a cherished job. Because these are "natural" parts of the human journey, we may not understand why we might feel adrift, sad, or depressed when faced with such events. We may need the help of others to see both the varied losses we are facing and their effects. Therefore, when listening pastorally to another, the minister must listen for the losses that may be present in the other's story, challenging the other and calling for healing. In listening for the loss, one may ask such questions as, "What has changed or been lost?" or "What do you fear might change or be lost?" One may also lift up for consideration one's sense of some losses that may be embedded in the other's story.

Third Sensitivity

Of course, we know that loss is a natural and inevitable part of life, and sometimes we may respond to loss with resilience, patience, and strength. While the loss may be difficult or painful, it does not ultimately challenge or shake our story. But sometimes our story can be rocked, threatened, or even destroyed in fundamental ways by loss. Such experiences of "narrative disruptions"[10] can be profoundly uncomfortable, and even terrifying. The story we have known and have been living can feel like it has fallen apart, and we can be left feeling like we are virtually outside of a story. Our sense of wholeness and well-being can be utterly destroyed. The effects of narrative disruption—if it fundamentally shakes our story and our sense of wholeness in the world—may be terribly painful and call for healing. Therefore, the third sensitivity that a minister can bring to compassionate pastoral listening is to *listen for the narrative disruption* that may have occurred. In listening for possible narrative disruption, the minister might ask such questions as, "What is happening to your life as you have known it?" "How do these losses affect the story of your life?" "Is your life story holding together, or are parts or all of it falling to pieces?"

Fourth Sensitivity

Why is narrative disruption potentially so challenging and painful? One way to understand this is to consider the connection between stories and meanings. Our story often conveys the meaning or meanings by which we live; therefore, disruption to one's story may also mean disruption to one's ways of making meaning. What do we mean by *meaning*? *Meaning* comes from the German root *meinen*, which means to think. Therefore, we can understand meaning as the ways we think about and understand life in general, and our lives in particular. Elsewhere, I have described meaning as "the deep sense we make of things, the way we understand the world, how we articulate the overarching purpose or goal of our lives, the significance we seek in living, the core values by which we order our lives."[11]

Meaning serves very important purposes for us. It creates an organizing structure for our story. It provides order and sense to how we think about life, and about our lives in particular. Meaning is deeply connected to our sense of wholeness. Without a sense of meaning, we can lack a sense of completeness, integrity, or well-being; life can feel utterly random, fragmented, and frightening. This is why disruptions to one's story can be so very painful; these disruptions can threaten or destroy the meaning or meanings that are embedded in one's story and help to create a sense of wholeness. Therefore, the fourth sensitivity I would like to propose for compassionate pastoral listening is to *listen for the meaning* that may have been shaken or threatened by loss. I believe that, in any ministry of care, it is often such shaken or threatened meaning that must be healed. I will say more about this later in the paper.

In listening for the meaning that may have been shaken or threatened by loss, ministers want to listen, in a particular way, for

182

theological meaning. That is, they want to listen for the ways people understand God's role in their lives and God's place in their suffering. For instance, someone may conclude that a loss is God's will or that the loss is God's punishment for some prior offense by the person. Another person may feel that God is lovingly present in the midst of suffering, while another may feel that God has abandoned him or her. Each of these perspectives articulates an important theological meaning that may have highly significant implications for one's relationship with God, and yet one may not be consciously aware of embracing such meaning. This is why it is essential that pastoral ministers listen for the meaning that may be deeply embedded in one's understanding of and response to suffering and loss. In listening for meaning, ministers might ask such questions as, "What do you think about all of this?" "What does all of this mean to you?" "Where is God in all of this?" "How do you understand God's presence and role in your loss and suffering?"

Listening on the Road to Emmaus

So far, I have described four sensitivities that pastoral ministers might bring to their compassionate listening: *listen for the story, listen for the loss, listen for the narrative disruption, and listen for the meaning.* I would now like to offer a reflection on a Gospel story in which we might imagine that the risen Christ models these sensitivities for us. Let us consider the beautiful Gospel story of the disciples on the Road to Emmaus (Luke 24:13–35).

This story is set just a few days after Jesus has been arrested, killed, and buried. Two disciples are walking to Emmaus, discussing all of these terrible events. We can easily imagine that they are utterly stunned, confused, sad, and perhaps terrified. They have experienced traumatic loss. Their beloved Messiah was shockingly ripped away from them and then killed in a most gruesome and painful way. They have lost their leader and even their leader's body. All aspects of their lives have been shaken. For instance, the ways they spent their days have been radically changed. They no longer have Jesus to follow, to talk with, to pray with, to eat with. The ways they imagined their futures—with Jesus present—have also been shaken to the core. The critical meanings by which the disciples were living their lives have come under fire. Jesus, "a prophet mighty in deed and word before God and all the people" (Luke 24:19), has been crucified, and yet "we had hoped that he was the one to redeem Israel" (Luke 24:21). From their perspective, it must seem that the story they were living has been horribly and irreparably changed; they are struggling with terrible narrative disruption, and the meanings that have undergirded their lives are all shaken and even decimated.

As they are talking with one another, the risen Christ appears and walks with them, although they do not recognize him. He asks them, "What are you discussing with each other while you walk along?" (Luke 24:17). Although Christ, of course, knows everything that has happened, he invites them to tell their story. At first they do not speak; "They stood still, looking sad" (Luke 24:17). Then one of them, Cleopas, asks in apparent surprise, if Christ is the only stranger in Jerusalem who does not know about these dramatic and horrifying events. Christ replies by asking, "What things?" (Luke 24:19), thereby inviting them a second time to tell their story. It is with this second invitation that the disciples begin to pour out their story of loss, narrative disruption, and shaken meaning. Through all of this, Christ listens. Imaginatively, we might say that Christ listens for the story, listens for the loss, listens for the narrative disruption, and listens for the meaning, for in fact, these are the very elements that the disciples share.

If the story ended there, Christ's interaction with the disciples would be a most moving example of compassionate listening. But Christ offers them something more: he offers them the possibility of hope in their suffering. He does this by recasting the painful events they have just described in light of scriptural references to himself. "Then he said to them, 'Oh, how foolish you are, and how slow of heart to believe all that the prophets have declared! Was it not necessary that the Messiah should suffer these things and then enter into his glory?' Then beginning with Moses and all the prophets, he interpreted to them the things about himself in all the scriptures" (Luke 24:25–27).

Through his words, Christ frees the disciples from understanding what has happened to him in terms only of horrible loss, narrative disruption, and shaken meaning. He offers them a new perspective that makes possible a hopeful stance in the face of loss. Christ offers them hope that the terrible events of recent days were not the end of their story. They have not lost their Messiah. The Messiah is with them now, which they recognize soon after in the Breaking of the Bread. We might imagine that this gift of hope in their terrible loss is what they are describing when they later ask, "Were not our hearts burning within us while he was talking to us on the road, while he was opening the scriptures to us?" (Luke 24:32).

Fifth Sensitivity

Christ offered the disciples the possibility of hope in their suffering. This has important implications for what pastoral ministers, too, are to offer others. Above, I proposed that when people are struggling in a deep or painful way, it is often shaken, shattered, or inadequate meaning that must be healed. A critical part of healing ministry, which claims Christ as its model, is to help others to find meaning in the midst of loss through the hope of the good news. As we have seen, the pastoral minister must listen for the other's story and for the loss, narrative disruption, and shaken meaning, which may be embedded therein. But for the Christian, these elements are never one's full story, nor are they ever the end of one's story. From a faith perspective, we know that each person's story continues to unfold in ultimately hopeful ways because of the constant, faithful, and active love of God in Christ.

Thus, a fifth sensitivity for compassionate listening is to *listen for the hope*. People often have an amazing capacity to hold onto hope, even in the midst of terrible loss, but sometimes they have trouble seeing this in themselves. Therefore, the pastoral minister listens for, lifts up, and supports the other's hope, helping the other to recognize and to reclaim the hope that grounds him or her in loss. In listening for hope, the minister might ask such questions as, "In what or in whom do you have hope right now?" or "As you imagine your future, what gives you hope?"

But sometimes people struggle to feel or find hope in the midst of their great pain, as perhaps did the disciples on the road to Emmaus. In this case, the role of the pastoral minister may be to *lend hope* to the other, as we might say, Christ did for the disciples; to remind the other that his or her story in Christ is not over, that our God is bigger than our losses, that our God is always present in love, beckoning us "into an open-ended future."[12] Having hope that our loving God is present in the midst of our suffering and calls us to a hopeful future is our greatest source both of meaning and of healing. This hope, while not minimizing or denying our suffering, allows us to move into God's open-ended future with trust that we are never alone in our suffering and that our lives might be whole again despite the great pain of loss. It is this hope that may allow us to feel that our hearts, like those of the disciples, are burning within us. Helping another to claim this hope is the greatest possible "evidence" that one's pastoral listening has offered healing in suffering.

What Does Pastoral Listening Require of the Minister?

Having considered these five sensitivities for compassionate pastoral listening and their critical role in healing, it is now time to ask, "What does this sort of pastoral listening require of the minister?" Some might say that this sort of pastoral listening that offers others the possibility of hope and healing in their struggles is an innate capacity that cannot be learned. I disagree. Just as I was able to hear the plane once my son made me aware of it, so I think we all have the potential to offer this sort of listening to others when we bring our minds and hearts to the privileged task. I would like to suggest three steps that ministers may take in order to grow more confident and more competent in this work.

First Step

First, compassionate pastoral listening requires that ministers embrace humility. There is no "one size fits all" blueprint for pastoral listening; each person's story and ways of making meaning are particular. Therefore, ministers must learn about the other, humbly and openly. They must surrender preordained ideas about the other's story and the other's world of meaning. They must learn where the other does, or might, find hope in his or her struggle. And they must accept humbly that their listening will always be limited, since God alone is the perfect listener.

This humble posture can be quite freeing for pastoral ministers. Sometimes ministers worry deeply about saying the right thing and being helpful to someone in distress. This worry can lead them to be preoccupied with the questions they should ask or the answers they should provide. As our own experience of sharing our story would likely suggest, what people often find most helpful is a much deeper and more open-ended sort of listening, in which pastoral ministers are truly open to what will emerge, without needing to know the answers or control the outcome. While perhaps scary in some ways, this humble posture of open listening can free ministers to be fully present both to others and to the ways God's spirit might be at work in their conversations.

Second Step

Second, compassionate pastoral listening requires that ministers cultivate both courage and wisdom. While particularly rich and rewarding, the sort of listening I have described can also be challenging and taxing. Ministers are often with people at difficult or even traumatic times and are listening for people's struggles with loss, narrative disruption, and threatened meaning. Ministers do not know where the pastoral conversation might go and, therefore, must be prepared to "ride the rapids" with the other. Ministers must also respond to people who may be struggling to feel or to find hope in their struggles. All of this requires courage.

This sort of listening also requires wisdom. First, ministers must have the wisdom to know that they are limited in what they can offer others. For example, sometimes ministers feel the terrible pressure to provide hope for those who may be struggling to feel any hope. Yet while ministers do their best to lend hope to such persons, ministers cannot, in fact, make others feel hope; they are limited. Rather they must point people to God, the ultimate source of hope for us all.

Trauma experts Lisa McCann and Laurie Anne Pearlman help us to understand a second aspect of the wisdom that pastoral listening requires. They describe how psychotherapists, who listen to the traumatic stories of clients, may over time, experience vicarious traumatization; that is, by listening over and over to others' traumatic experiences, psychotherapists risk being traumatized themselves.[13] So it may also be with pastoral ministers. Listening to the stories, the losses, the narrative disruptions, and the threatened meanings of others may shake the minister's own sense of stability and safety. Pastoral ministers must have the wisdom to know both when they can move into such challenging territory and when they may need to pull back in order to take care of themselves and protect against excessive destabilization of self. Sometimes a minister may not be able to listen well to another, and it is important to recognize such moments and to respond in ways (e.g., by referral to another pastoral minister) that care for both the minister and the other.

Third Step

Third, offering compassionate pastoral listening to others requires that the ministers, too, have experienced the compassionate pastoral listening of others. It is very difficult to offer others what we ourselves have not received. Ministers, like those they wish to serve, know loss, narrative disruption, and threatened meaning. Ministers, too, need hope in their suffering. Ministers need to know that others suffer with them; that is, they need to receive the compassionate listening of others. Thus, ministers must ask themselves, "Can I share my own story of loss, of narrative disruption, and threatened meaning with others? Can I receive the compassionate care of others? Can I allow others to suffer with me?"

If ministers have not had sufficient experience of receiving this sort of compassionate listening, they want actively to cultivate this experience for themselves. Spiritual direction is a wonderful opportunity to experience deep listening by one's spiritual director or guide, whose focus is on the story one is telling and how God may be present therein. Many people value counseling or therapy as another important way to experience the focused listening of another in the midst of one's suffering or searching. Through these means and others, ministers may come to a deeper, fuller sense of others' suffering with them, offering them compassion and care. And this will nourish them as they offer compassionate listening to others.

Of course, ministers must ultimately be nourished and sustained in this ministry by our Listening God, in whose name they offer pastoral listening to others.[14] Ministers need to know and trust that our Listening God listens to them as well, suffering with them and offering them hope in their struggles. Depending on their own life stories, some ministers may struggle at times to know and trust that God listens with love and compassion not only to others but to them as well. Therefore, they may need to take steps—and perhaps take risks—to let God into their lives more fully. Spiritual direction, retreats, and individual and communal prayer can deepen their sense of connection with our Listening God. Sharing more deeply of themselves and receiving the pastoral listening of others can also serve this purpose. Through such means, and through God's gracious activity in their lives, they may come to an ever-fuller sense of God listening faithfully, offering precisely the compassion, the hope, and the healing that they most need.

Notes

1. See etymology of compassion on, for example, www. etymonline.com; www.thefreedictionary.com; www.merriam-webster.com/dictionary (accessed on 11/9/11).

2. Nicholas Wolterstorff, *Lament for a Son* (Grand Rapids: Eerdmans, 1987), 63.

3. Scripture quotations are taken from the *New Revised Standard Bible*, copyright © 1989 by the Division of Christian Education of the National Council of Churches of Christ in the USA. Used by permission. All rights reserved.

4. See, for example, Matthew 9:36, 14:14, 15:32, 20:34; Mark 6:34, 8:2; Luke 7:13.

5. Susan K. Hedahl, *Listening Ministry: Rethinking Pastoral Leadership* (Minneapolis: Fortress Press, 2001), xii.

6. From www.thefreedictionary.com/healing (accessed on 11/9/11). Also see definitions of "healing" on www.etymonline. com and www.merriam-webster.com/dictionary (accessed on 11/9/11).

7. For a fuller treatment of stories in human experience, see, for example, Dan P. McAdams, *The Stories We Live By: Personal Myths and the Making of the Self* (New York: William Morrow, 1993) and Donald E. Polkinghorne, *Narrative Knowing and the Human Sciences* (Albany: State University of New York Press, 1988).

8. Katie G. Cannon and others, *God's Fierce Whimsy* (New York: Pilgrim, 1985), 133.

9. Kenneth R. Mitchell and Herbert Anderson, *All Our Losses, All Our Griefs* (Philadelphia: Westminster, 1983).

10. Robert A. Neimeyer, "Narrative Disruptions in the Construction of the Self," in *Constructions of Disorder: Meaning-Making Frameworks for Psychotherapy*, ed. Robert A. Neimeyer and Jonathan D. Raskin (Washington, DC: American Psychological Association, 2000), 207.

11. Melissa Kelley, *Grief: Contemporary Theory and the Practice of Ministry* (Minneapolis, MN: Fortress Press, 2010), 75.

12. Andrew Lester, *Hope in Pastoral Care and Counseling* (Louisville, KY: Westminster John Knox, 1995), 2.

13. Lisa McCann and Laurie Anne Pearlman, "Vicarious Traumatization: A Framework for Understanding the Psychological Effects of Working with Victims," *Journal of Traumatic Stress* 3 (1990): 131–49.

14. Susan Hedahl describes the pastoral listener as offering "incarnational listening," trying to manifest something of the Divine presence to the other through the very act of listening, in Susan K. Hedahl, *Listening Ministry: Rethinking Pastoral Leadership* (Minneapolis: Fortress Press, 2001), 99.

12

HEALING BROKENNESS IN MULTICULTURAL COMMUNITIES OF FAITH

Hosffman Ospino

To be Catholic in the United States in the twenty-first century is to be part of an experience of profound transformations. Transformation implies change, and change brings along a mixture of feelings of brokenness and hope. This, of course, is not the first time that U.S. Catholicism faces major transformations in its short history. Neither it will be the last, as long as we continue to be a community of faith, renewed by the constant presence of migrants from around the world and seeking to authentically respond to the challenges of living in a complex society like ours. It is at the parish level where communities are being profoundly transformed, particularly as many of them become multicultural communities of faith. Where do we stand in the face of this transformation: brokenness or hope? This chapter is a pastoral theological reflection on the challenges of becoming a multicultural parish and a guide to building community in the midst of diversity. For some Catholics in multicultural parishes, brokenness is the prevailing feeling as they see their communities become something new. For other Catholics in those same communities, the prevailing feeling is that of hope because the multicultural community is their new home, and that is where they now belong. Even for others, hope is possible because they are engaged in a process of forging new ways of being Church. The goal of this reflection is to ultimately invite Catholics in multicultural communities of faith to turn brokenness into hope as part of a healing process.

Before we proceed, it is necessary that we define three key concepts that will appear frequently in this reflection: multicultural community of faith, brokenness, and hope. First, a multicultural community of faith is understood here mainly as a parish that welcomes faithful from various cultural traditions to celebrate the mysteries of the Christian faith in their own languages and traditions. Although there are communities of faith that transcend the structures of the parish and share similar criteria of cultural diversity (e.g., ecclesial movements, prayer groups, associations of faithful, missions), most of the time these communities are associated with local parishes. Second, brokenness is defined as the feeling of losing something that, at some point, was perceived to provide meaning as an integrated whole.[1] Brokenness may be the result of a sudden loss or the perception that things are not as they used to be, which can reveal a rather idealized assessment of the past. Third, hope is understood here as a human drive to expect the "best" out of a situation with the pre-understanding that this "best" is real and achievable. In this sense, hope is beyond ideology and utopia.[2] From a Christian perspective, hope has an even more profound meaning when it is contemplated as a theological virtue, a gift of the Holy Spirit through which we possess in anticipation—although not definitively—that which we hope for: "It is the expectation of things to come from the perspective of a present that is already given. It is a looking-forward in Christ's presence, with Christ who is present, to the perfecting of his Body, to his definitive coming."[3]

The Emergence of the Multicultural Community of Faith

Diversity is not a foreign experience for Christians. Already in the Book of Acts, the first disciples addressed issues of diversity vis-à-vis language, ethnicity, culture, and particular interpretations of Jewish and Christian identity.[4] In the United States, no Catholic group has avoided the challenges of cultural diversity. This is so because Catholicism—and Christianity in general in this country—is primarily an "immigrant" religious experience: immigrant because it came to the U.S. territory with Catholic missionaries and colonizers from other lands; immigrant because it became established under the efforts of different Catholic groups that arrived from different parts of the world; immigrant because it has been constantly renewed by migration waves that bring new perspectives and new life to the idea of being a U.S. Catholic.[5] The responses to cultural diversity at the local level have varied. At some moments, missions served as the best solution; at others, it was the development of national parishes; today, we witness the widespread phenomenon of multicultural parishes.

Thousands of national parishes served the needs of European Catholic immigrants for most of the nineteenth and twentieth centuries. As the first generation of European Catholic immigrants passed and their descendants became more assimilated into the larger U.S. culture, English became the common language for most. At the same time, U.S. Catholicism entered into a process of developing its own cultural identity in a rather complex conversation with the larger American culture.[6] Catholic parishes with mostly Caucasian, English-speaking parishioners embraced models of community life that dominated the idea of being Catholic in the United States. It must be said that African-American, Asian-American, Hispanic, and Native American Catholics, for various socio-historical reasons beyond the focus of this analysis, did not always follow similar the patterns of parish organization compared to their Euro-American counterparts. However, in the second part of the twentieth century, a new migration wave (still ongoing) mostly from Latin America—although with a significant number of immigrants from Asia and some African countries—was to transform the Catholic experience in the United States. Millions of these immigrants, particularly those from Latin America, are Catholic. Approximately seventy percent of the growth of the Catholic Church in our country during the last five decades is the result of the increasing Hispanic presence.[7] Where are these Catholics?

In order to respond to this question, we need to name three realities that have coincided in recent decades. First, the 1983 Code of Canon Law introduced the personal parish as a canonical structure, an ecclesiastical unit to be "determined by reason of the rite, language, or nationality of the Christian faithful of some territory, or even for some other reason."[8] Personal parishes exist in various parts of the United States, but very few are established explicitly to serve ethnic groups. The structure of national parishes has, by and large, disappeared as a regular way of serving the needs of ethnic communities. The majority of these national parishes, except those that have closed, have become territorial parishes. Most ethnic groups, today, find a home in the territorial parish. Second, the latest immigration wave has coincided with the rapid decline in numbers of Euro-American Catholics, millions of whom have ceased to identify with the Catholic Church or simply do not practice their faith with the larger community. Millions of Catholic immigrants are filling in the spaces[9] left by those Catholics who are not active in the Church any longer.[10] Third, as the number of Catholics from various ethnicities grows, dioceses around the country have responded by developing the model of multicultural parishes, communities where two or three—sometimes more—ethnic and/or linguistic communities coincide. Sometimes these multicultural parishes emerge in natural ways as pastors and their pastoral staffs seek to meet the spiritual needs of all Catholics living in the parish territory. Other communities become the de facto multicultural community for the diocese where ethnic groups are assigned.

Returning to our question (where are the "new" Catholics?), the answer is evident. Many practice their faith and live their Catholic identity in the context of territorial parishes that are transitioning from a mostly Euro-American population to one that is mostly Hispanic or Asian or African; many practice their faith and live their Catholic identity in the context of multicultural parishes, whether constituted naturally, as described above, or designated as such by the local bishop. As of 2011, there are approximately 17,800 Catholic parishes in the United States.[11] Nearly a third of these parishes (5,500) have explicitly developed some form of Hispanic Ministry; hundreds more serve Asian and Pacific Island Catholics as well as Catholic immigrants from Africa. Without a doubt, the U.S. Catholic experience in the twenty-first century is being shaped by the dynamic of the multicultural community of faith, a dynamic that is simultaneously a source of brokenness and hope. The first step toward healing—understood here as transition from brokenness to hope—is to name the ways in which brokenness is experienced by many Catholics in these communities, while envisioning some glimpses of hope toward which we turn our gazes as women and men of faith.

Between Brokenness and Hope

The experience of sharing and celebrating our Christian faith in the context of a multicultural community can be profoundly life-giving. This certainly requires a level of preparedness and openness to appreciate difference as well as becoming comfortable with the idea of change. Nevertheless, many Christians in our communities are not prepared to hold either perspective. This is not necessarily anyone's fault; it is simply how we have come to understand life in the parish over the years. Let us name three dynamics that often lead to communal brokenness in the context of multicultural communities of faith and envision the hopes that can help us make such communities of faith stronger.

The first dynamic is shaped by a tension between "locals" and "newcomers." Catholic parishes, by and large, are stable ecclesiastical units that serve the spiritual needs—as well as other basic human needs—primarily of those who live in their territory. In each community, we encounter core groups of parishioners whose lives of faith have been intimately linked to their parishes: there they were initiated into the Christian faith, have married, and have been spiritually sustained over the years. Their parents and grandparents had a similar experience. Some of their children will do likewise. These core Catholic parishioners have a unique sense of ownership of the parish. They have been there for generations; their ancestors—literally—built the structures; the parish, in many ways, is *their* community. But many of these parishes have become multicultural communities of faith and have undergone significant demographic changes. Demographic transitions are often triggered by migratory mobility in a globalized world, or by the fact that younger families constantly move in search for better jobs, or simply by the shifting socio-economic conditions of any given locality, among other factors.[12] Newcomers arrive in these parishes, searching for a home to share and celebrate the same faith of the locals. In this sense, both groups have something in common. But the newcomers lack the historical rootedness and the sense of belonging of the more established group; they bring their own traditions and perspectives as to how faith is celebrated. Tension builds. On the one hand, the locals are inclined to hold on to their own ways ("this is how we have always done it here") and expect that the newcomers assimilate into what they have. On the other hand, the newcomers also bring their own ways ("this is how we did it somewhere else") and expect that things change to accommodate their perspectives as well as their most immediate needs. When the differences are not appropriately addressed and when the tensions become insurmountable, multicultural communities can experience a massive exodus on both sides, thus risking the actual stability of the community.

Healing this instance of communal brokenness must lead to the hope of building a community where locals and newcomers share the parish as a common home, a home that belongs to everyone, a home that is not yet finished. This does not mean that differences need to be erased or that one group has to assimilate into the other's ways. Tensions about difference will always exist, and they must be on the table as we interact with one another. Healing, in this situation, requires the embrace of Christian hope through which we acknowledge that we already possess, in some sense, what we hope for. In other words, as baptized Christians and disciples of Jesus Christ, we already share the same calling to be saved, we are already children of the same God, and we are already members of Christ's Body, the Church.

The second dynamic is shaped by how we understand "otherness." Every personal interaction, whether with a close friend or with someone of whom we know little, is constituted by a basic relationship: *I* and the *other*.[13] The "I," that is to say my own conscious, personal self through whom I become present in the world, is aware that there is someone else whose life has infinite value and shares in rather distinct ways my most immediate reality. The "other," also a conscious, personal self—who is not me—is the person with whom I relate, the person whose presence makes me aware of my own selfhood, the person whose existence imposes a responsibility upon me simply because she/he exists.[14] Just as the *other* is an "other" to me, I am an "other" to her/him. In the community we speak of "we" and "others." We both participate in the experience of otherness, which cannot be ignored because we both share a common historical and existential reality. Being Christians in multicultural communities of faith places us before a twofold challenge. On the one hand, we are called to recognize the face of Christ in the others around us, regardless of their language, ethnicity, or socio-historical circumstances. This requires an exercise of transcending difference. On the other hand, we must come to terms with the fact that it is factors, such as, language, ethnicity, and socio-historical location (to mention only a few), which profoundly shape the otherness of the people with whom we share life in community. This requires an exercise of affirming difference. Transcending and affirming difference of what makes others *other* is essential to building inclusive and life-giving communities of faith. Both attitudes need to go hand in hand; though different, they are not mutually exclusive. Brokenness in the context of the multicultural community of faith, then, occurs when difference is perceived as an obstacle to affirm what is important or when difference is dismissed by a biased sense of unity (i.e., homogeneity, assimilation). If others are narrowly defined, for instance, as those who simply are not like us or those whose presence is threatening because of their differences or those whose particular ways challenge the status quo with which we are comfortable, brokenness will prevail and the community can dissolve.

Healing this instance of communal brokenness must lead to the hope of affirming otherness and difference in light of the gospel message. God made all women and men in the divine image and likeness (Gen 1:27), and thus, our dignity is deeply rooted in this common origin. In Jesus Christ, humanity (with all our differences), is called to a new and definitive relationship with God. Because God loves us infinitely through Jesus Christ, Christians must actualize that love in all our relationships. At the most basic level, the *I* is called to love the *other* with the love that God loves us in Jesus Christ. Our hope is sustained upon the double conviction that God made us capable of loving with divine love (charity) and that we have already experienced the fullness of God's love in Jesus Christ. When we love others, we love them for who they are—images of God and heirs of God's divine salvation—and we affirm the differences that make them unique. Needless to say, this is an inversely reciprocal relationship.

The third dynamic is related to the experience of hospitality. When building communities of faith, we either stand as hospitable hosts or as beneficiaries of love that is embracing and welcoming. In the community of faith, some welcome; others are welcomed. This is part of a relational continuum that is necessary to renew communities. If the continuum ends, the community simply ceases to exist.[15] To speak of hospitality is even more demanding when the other, the newcomer, is a flesh-and-blood person who is here to form community with us, in our own church, our own home—not merely someone who lives at a distance or someone whom we imagine. Let's remember that our focus here is on those multicultural communities of faith where Christians from different cultural backgrounds already coexist.[16] "Locals" are faced with the responsibility of practicing their faith convictions by opening their community (and their hearts!) to the stranger.[17] But there is also some responsibility on the part of "newcomers," not only to accept the hospitality offered to them, but also to reciprocate it. It is a two-way dynamic. In the midst of this dynamic, three related questions emerge: One, how much hospitality do "locals" need to offer? Two, how much hospitality can "newcomers" expect—or demand? Three, what kind of hospitality is expected from women and men who claim to be disciples of Jesus Christ? Addressing each of these questions would require a new chapter, perhaps a book. Let us assert for now that these questions point to three tensions that, in the context of the multicultural parish, could be sources of communal brokenness. First, established communities often debate whether they should offer some form of "radical" or "pure" hospitality that welcomes everyone, no questions asked, regardless of their backgrounds and intentions.[18] Although such hospitality acknowledges the other as a gift and affirms the infinite value of every person, the community is also conscious that this hospitality demands a vulnerability that opens the possibility of being transformed in radical ways—positively or negatively. The key issue here is whether hospitality has limits and how these limits are determined. Second, newcomers, for the most part, are faced with the unknown character of the context in which they find themselves. Their experience of hospitality often depends on the structures and policies that communities have set in place to welcome them, affirm their gifts, and grant them enough agency to develop their identity in the new context. As the newcomers settle into the life of the community, thanks to the hospitality of which they partake, there begins a gradual negotiation of the terms of such hospitality. Conflicts can emerge when newcomers eventually do not see themselves as such anymore and begin to act like locals, when they feel that life in the community can be different, or when the community itself demands more commitment on their part. Third, Christians are informed by the principles of the gospel, which as a source of spiritual wisdom, provides directions for building communities of faith. Nonetheless, in the building of the multicultural community of faith, Christians may realize that the gospel sometimes does not provide sufficient clarity about the many issues that emerge on a day-to-day basis, or that it makes demands for hospitality that the community of believers may not be yet ready to embrace (e.g., welcoming the utterly marginalized into one's community/home; loving one's enemies; giving to Caesar what is Caesar's and to God what is God's).

Healing this instance of communal brokenness starts with the contemplation of God's example of divine hospitality, which leads us to the hope of actualizing it in our own midst. God calls humanity to participate in the divine life, and more specifically to salvation in Jesus Christ. Hospitality has a salvific dimension. God's example of divine hospitality is a vocation that helps us to live our humanity to the fullest; God's example of divine hospitality is a free and gratuitous gift. God models for us an example of hospitality that, in many ways, we can describe as radical. But radical here does not mean impossible. It is possible insofar as we know that God has already allowed us to experience it (we know what it is to be welcomed and loved by God), and God guides us with the gifts of the Holy Spirit to actualize it in the context of our communities. Moreover, God's radical hospitality is possible because, in becoming the ultimate guest, the perfect gift to humanity in Jesus Christ, God allowed us to embrace the *Other* into our own lives despite our limitations. Just us we are capable of extending hospitality to the ultimate *Other*, so must we do to the *others*, the newcomers whom we meet every day in our multi-cultural communities of faith.

Seven Strategies to Heal Brokenness in Multicultural Communities of Faith

How do we begin a process of healing that leads from brokenness to realized hope? There is no magic formula. Our communities are constituted by flesh-and-blood human beings, gifted yet limited. However, as Christians, we are people of faith who must trust the work of the Holy Spirit in our lives and our communities. God's Spirit will guide us, but we must do our part. The following seven strategies constitute a guide to healing communities of faith rooted in the Christian experience, particularly in culturally diverse contexts. These strategies are rather practical and must be read in light of the reflections delineated in the previous two sections.

Strategy 1: *(Re)Define the Parish in Constructive, Life-Giving Terms*

The territorial parish is the dominant model of Catholic community of faith in the United States. This model is largely defined by the Code of Canon Law as an ecclesiastical unit in the local church, namely the diocese, entrusted by the bishop to the pastoral care of a pastor.[19] This definition of the Catholic parish is useful insofar as it helps us to understand the parish as part of a larger structure and provides the criteria for its administration. Nevertheless, the canonical definition of the parish does not necessarily imply that parishes are homogeneous and static communities. Parishes enjoy a remarkable diversity that makes them vibrant communities of faith where people search for God, learn about their faith, worship, and serve one another. The people who come to these communities are significantly diverse in terms of their age, socioeconomic status, political perspectives, and spiritual journeys, to name only a few. The growth of ecclesial movements nationwide is infusing parishes with new life. Small ecclesial communities continue to bring Christians closer to the scriptures and to a better understanding of Christian discipleship. In multicultural parishes, we encounter added factors, such as, cultural and linguistic diversity. The Catholic parish is, rather, a context where various communities coincide. It is then imperative that we envision metaphors and models of parish life that transcend the canonical definition of parish and affirm the richness of experiences in the lives of the people who constitute them. One such model is the parish as "community of communities."[20]

Strategy 2: *Acknowledge That We Are at a Crossroads*

The presence of new faces and voices in our communities of faith is an invitation to rethink our own communal identity. Historically, Catholic parishes have responded—and continue to respond—in various ways to the presence of "newcomers," especially those who speak a different language or those who are of a different ethnic background in comparison to the most established groups. In some cases, the response was rejection: early in the twentieth century, African-Americans were prohibited from attending services in many parishes where mostly "white" Catholics worshiped. Some communities have adopted monolingual policies (e.g., "only-English") for their worship services and faith formation programs to force assimilation or to establish some distance from those who do not speak the language. In other cases, the presence of newcomers has triggered the "flight" of the more established parishioners, thus weakening the life of the parish, particularly in urban settings. In other cases, the response has been some form of integration. Mindful of past mistakes and aware of the current challenges that U.S. Catholics face in the twenty-first century, rejection and marginalization must be ruled out as options. There is enough evidence to say that both are immoral and opposite to the Christian message. Catholic communities of faith are at a crossroads. On the one hand, we are aware that our parishes are undergoing dramatic transformations in terms of demographics and cultural perspectives; that parishes are in constant flux; that integration takes time and patience; that models that work in one parish may not work at another. On the other hand, we need to respond soon to those challenges. Rather than hiding, ignoring, or fleeing from this reality, we must acknowledge its complexity and address it with creativity. After all, these are our communities.

Strategy 3: *Develop a Politics of Reconciliation*

Life in community requires structures that facilitate reconciliation. Without such structures, the community is bound to experience division, suffering, injustice, and ultimately chaos. Multicultural Christian communities of faith can embrace what some contemporary political philosophers call a "politics of reconciliation."[21] The presence of multiple voices in the community has enormous potential to enrich everyone, whether as individuals or as groups, with multiple perspectives about the issues that bring the community together. However, communal dialogue and cohesion cannot exist unless the community addresses the brokenness resulting from the various tensions described in the previous section. From the perspective of a politics of reconciliation, members of the community—more particularly its leaders—must come to the table of dialogue where voices are recognized, affirmed, and listened to. *Recognition* is crucial, not as mere tolerance or tokenism, but as an authentic affirmation of the value of the other. Once the other is recognized as a constitutive member of the larger whole, the community must seek to develop just structures of *inclusiveness* that guarantee participation. If those structures do not exist, the community must create them. It is only when all members of the community are recognized and know themselves part of the whole (inclusion) that brokenness can turn into hope. As Christians, we have the advantage of building on our faith convictions to structure communal life in ways that are life-giving and reconciling. Besides the political arrangements that we can create with our human efforts to build communities of faith, we must also draw from the Gospel to set the parameters of reconciliation: God's ultimate gesture of reconciling love to humanity is Jesus Christ, the Word made flesh, who became one of us to give us eternal life (John 3:16); no greater sign identifies the disciple of Christ than love (John 13:34–35); where two or three are gathered, the Lord is in their midst (Matt 18:20); one cannot offer a gift to God unless one is reconciled with the other (Matt 5:23–24); the face of the other, particularly the one who is most in need, is the face of Christ (Matt 25:31–46).

Strategy 4: *Start with What We Already Have: Symbols and Stories*

When multicultural communities of faith engage in processes of healing—namely to transition from brokenness into hope—one of the most common questions is: where do we start? Sometimes we search for "what worked" in other communities and take those experiences as if they were universal formulas applicable to any similar situation. Other times, we might rely on the advice of outside experts who may offer valuable wisdom. Both strategies can work to a certain extent, but more likely, they will fall short from what the community actually needs. Conventional wisdom tells us that "all politics are local" and so we could paraphrase saying that "all communal healing is local." The experience of other communities can play an important role in the process of healing brokenness in multicultural parishes and so can the wisdom of those who have studied these realities. But perhaps the most valuable resources that these communities have to move toward healing are the symbols and the stories of the people who constitute them. They are already there; they are not prepackaged. Every cultural group possesses symbols and stories that powerfully capture how they understand what it means to be human and what it means to be in relationship with others and

God. Every cultural group has stories that capture their struggles and hopes. Healing cannot occur if those symbols and stories are ignored. In sharing them, people discover that they have more in common than they imagined. Sharing their symbols and stories, "locals" tell "newcomers" about their roots, what they cherish most, how they have come to be who they are, and even their fears. Sharing their symbols and stories, "newcomers" tell "locals" about their journeys, their hopes, what they bring to the community, and also their fears. When symbols and stories are shared with one another, they become the symbols and stories of the community, our symbols and our stories.

Strategy 5: *The Power of Ritual*

Authentic Christian life is sustained by prayer and worship. In prayer, the members of the community enter into a transforming conversation with God and with one another as one family guided by the Holy Spirit that empowers us to say *Abba* (Rom 8:15). In the multicultural community of faith, prayer is mediated by the various cultural perspectives through which its members interpret the Christian faith: language, music, narratives, gestures, and symbols. The diversity of these expressions enriches the life of prayer and worship of the community. To expect that only one language or one symbol or one particular ritual should exhaust the fullness of the Christian religious experience in the multicultural community is rather naïve. This even applies to the celebration of the Eucharist, where unity is uniquely expressed through worship. The Second Vatican Council Constitution on the Sacred Liturgy affirms: "Even in the liturgy, the Church has no wish to impose a rigid uniformity in matters which do not implicate the faith or the good of the whole community; rather does she respect and foster the genius and talents of the various races and peoples."[22] Part of being Catholic Christians is to perceive the world as a sacramental reality, where God is in constant relationship with us and can be reached in many ways. Ritual allows us to actualize that relationship in the everyday. But we cannot separate ritual—or the ability to ritualize our faith—from our human experience, which is always shaped by culture. Thus, the process of healing brokenness in multicultural communities of faith must take into consideration the many rituals (e.g., popular Catholicism, devotions, family celebrations) as valid resources to learn, not only how people from different cultures enter in relationship with God, but also how they understand the mystery of being human in the everyday.

Strategy 6: *Nurture a Communal Perspective*

It is perfectly normal that various interests coincide in the context of multicultural communities of faith. Some members feel called to sustain the community by exercising leadership and sharing central values that provide a common identity. Sometimes this requires establishing necessary boundaries and envisioning projects that facilitate the growth of the community. Other members are interested in meeting the most immediate needs of specific groups: children, youth, the sick, the elderly, parents, etc. Members of particular immigrant, ethnic, or linguistic groups are often concerned about affirming and passing on the symbols, stories, and traditions that sustain the faith of entire families. The coexistence of this variety of interests offers a very important challenge to all members of the multicultural community of faith: to maintain a healthy balance between the particular and the general. Or more exactly, to honor the individual perspectives of the particular groups while nurturing a communal perspective that puts all these interests at the service of building the larger ecclesial body. Without a communal (ecclesial) perspective, communities are weakened by conflicts of interest, which will inevitably lead to painful brokenness. The coexistence of multiple interests is what makes the community of faith a diverse and vibrant reality. The Apostle Paul reminds us that "whatever is true, whatever is honorable, whatever is just, whatever is pure, whatever is pleasing, whatever is commendable, if there is any excellence and if there is anything worthy of praise, think about these things" (Phil

4:8). It is these things that make unity possible amidst diversity. They serve as helpful criteria through which the Christian community discerns the various interests that coincide within it. If the interests are true, honorable, just, pure, pleasing, commendable, excellent, and worthy of praise, then they should be embraced by the whole community of faith. A communal perspective ultimately depends on the gift of communal discernment.

Strategy 7: *Openness to Grace*

At the end of the day, when all is said and done to make our multicultural communities of faith better places where brokenness is no more and hope is realized in some way, Christians must rely on God's divine grace. We have the privilege of living in a culture that leads the way in matters related to organizational theory, business practices, and managerial strategies. There is a lot that we can learn from these fields to make the day-to-day dynamics of our parishes more effective. Much from these fields can be implemented to facilitate conversations, to improve our human interactions, and to address practical issues that may be the cause of communal brokenness. Yet we must never lose sight that our communities of faith are not just secular organizations or businesses. Parishes are ecclesial communities constituted by women and men—of all cultural backgrounds—that share a common faith, a sense of being called by God (i.e., vocation) to be what they are, and whose main purpose is to make possible that women and men everywhere experience God's salvific love in Jesus Christ. Because God calls many of us to be Church in the particular context of the multicultural community of faith, Christians must open ourselves to God's grace and the guidance of the Holy Spirit. Grace heals and transforms; grace makes us new. This, of course, does not mean that we should stop doing everything we can to facilitate healing where there is brokenness in our communities. We must do our part, using all resources available to us: *gratia supponit naturam* (grace builds on nature). Nonetheless, we also know as women and men of faith that *gra-*

tia elevat naturam (grace elevates nature). Openness to grace in the process of healing brokenness in the multicultural community of faith requires that we maintain both dynamics in healthy tension.

Conclusion

Catholicism in the twenty-first century is being defined by life in the multicultural parish. We cannot close our eyes to this reality or ignore the impact of cultural diversity in the way in which we live and celebrate our faith in the United States. As we reflected in this chapter, life in the multicultural community of faith can be accompanied by instances of brokenness that need healing. There are always glimpses of hope toward which we move; hope that, in one way or another, we already possess as women and men of faith. Multicultural parishes must develop the ability of becoming spaces (oases) of reconciliation and hope. May the seven strategies proposed in this reflection serve as a starting point for dialogue, healing, and the fashioning of true Catholic communities of faith; where everyone, with all our cultural backgrounds, is welcomed.

Notes

1. The concept "integrated whole" should be used with caution. It should be understood more as a coherent set of relationships and agreed upon conventions rather than a finished product. For instance, a monoethnic and monolinguistic parish, in a suburban context, can be deemed an integrated whole both culturally and ecclesiastically, yet it is always a complex reality in terms of leadership, generational differences, and socioeconomic dynamics.

2. *Ou-topia* is rather a place that does not exist, an ideal that in essence is not achievable. However, there is a way to rescue the concept "utopia" within the context of Christian hope: God's reign has been promised to us. It is a reign of justice and love; it is a good place (*eu-topia*) to live, which has been inaugurated by

Jesus Christ. It is the conviction that the place of the good exists that makes hope possible in the midst of brokenness and injustice. See Jon Sobrino, *No Salvation Outside the Poor: Prophetic-Utopia Essays* (Maryknoll, NY: Orbis Books, 2008), 80–82.

3. Pope Benedict XVI, *Saved in Hope: Spe Salvi* (Vatican City: Libreria Editrice Vaticana, 2007), 9.

4. See Acts 6 (the election of deacons); Acts 10 (the Holy Spirit comes to the Gentiles); Acts 15 (the Council of Jerusalem).

5. For a detailed historical analysis of the Catholic immigrant perspective in the United States, see Jay P. Dolan, *The American Catholic Experience: A History from Colonial Times to The Present* (Garden City, NY: Image Books, 1987); Allen Figueroa Deck, *The Second Wave: Hispanic Ministry and The Evangelization of Cultures* (New York, NY: Paulist Press, 1989).

6. See, for instance, Mark Massa and Catherine Osborne, eds., *American Catholic History: A Documentary Reader* (New York, NY: New York University, 2008); Mark Massa, *Catholics and American Culture: Fulton Sheen, Dorothy Day, and the Notre Dame Football Team* (New York, NY: Crossroad Publishing Co., 1999).

7. For relevant statistics about recent migration trends transforming the U.S. Catholic experience, see Peter C. Phan and Diana Hayes, eds., *Many Faces, One Church: Cultural Diversity and the American Catholic Experience* (Lanham, MD: Rowman & Littlefield, 2005), 1–11.

8. *Code of Canon Law*, c. 518.

9. This reality explains, in part, the fact that recent Catholic immigrants and their descendants are not faced with the immediate challenge of erecting new church buildings.

10. Let us keep in mind that, as the children and grandchildren of the latest wave of Catholic immigrants becomes more assimilated into the larger culture, they tend to embrace patterns of indifferentism and defection that should be of concern to pastoral leaders in the Church. A case in point is the reality of Hispanic youth. See Ken Johnson-Mondragón, ed., *Pathways of Hope and Faith among Hispanic Teens: Pastoral Reflections and Strategies Inspired by the National Study of Youth and Religion* (Stockton, CA: Instituto Fe y Vida, 2007), 20–23, 88, 94–97, 272–73.

11. See Mark M. Gray, Mary L. Gautier, and Melissa A. Cidade, *The Changing Face of U.S. Catholic Parishes* (Washington, DC: National Association for Lay Ministry (NALM), Emerging Models of Pastoral Leadership Project, 2011). Available online at http://emergingmodels.org/files/2012/04/Changing-Face-of-US-Catholic-Parishes.pdf (accessed September 13, 2012).

12. For an interesting analysis on the impact of social mobility in U.S. culture and its impact on the practice of religion, see Nancy T. Ammerman, "Work, Family, and the Churches: Where Are We and Where Can We Go?" *Word & World* 17, no. 4 (Fall 1997): 358–64. Also see Carl S. Dudley and Nancy T. Ammerman, *Congregations in Transition* (San Francisco, CA: Jossey Bass, 2002).

13. Jewish philosopher Martin Buber would speak of *I and Thou*. See Martin Buber, *I and Thou*, trans. Walter Kaufmann (New York, NY: Scribner, 1970).

14. See Emmanuel Levinas, "Martin Buber and the Theory of Knowledge," in *The Levinas Reader*, ed. Seán Hand, 66–67 (Oxford, UK: Blackwell, 1989).

15. Communities that fail to welcome new voices and perspectives risk isolation, irrelevance, and ultimately disappearance.

16. Because of this, our reflection goes beyond contemplating to open the community to someone else or to determine the criteria for hospitality toward someone who is to come. Both are, rather, preceding stages of a reflection that many communities cannot have because they *are* already multicultural. It would be ideal that communities of faith actually had the time to reflect and prepare to transition into culturally diverse bodies, yet most multicultural parishes find themselves addressing, in their reflections, what they have become.

17. The Greek term in the New Testament for hospitality in English is *philoxenia*: love for the stranger. See Rom 12:13; Heb 13:2.

18. Philosopher Jacques Derrida refers to the idea of "unconditional" hospitality as "a welcome without reserve and without calculation, an exposure without limit to whoever arrives." Jacques Derrida, "Principle of Hospitality," *Parallax* 11, no. 1 (2005): 6. The idea is radical and quite attractive in principle, yet it borders the limits of impossibility. On the issue of hospitality,

see Letty M. Russell, *Just Hospitality: God's Welcome in a World of Difference*, ed. J. Shannon Clarkson and Kate M. Ott (Louisville, KY: Westminster John Knox Press, 2009); Arthur Sutherland, *I Was a Stranger: A Christian Theology of Hospitality* (Nashville, TN: Abingdon Press, 2006). On hospitality, from the perspective of a theology of religions, see *Hospitality and the Other: Pentecost, Christian Practices, and the Neighbor* (Maryknoll, NY: Orbis Books, 2008).

19. See *Code of Canon Law*, c. 516.

20. See Hosffman Ospino, "Rethinking the Urban Parish in Light of the New Catholicity," *New Theology Review* 21, no. 1 (February 2008).

21. See Will Kymlicka and Bashir Bashir, eds., *The Politics of Reconciliation in Multicultural Societies* (Oxford, UK: Oxford University Press, 2008).

22. Second Vatican Council, Constitution on the Sacred Liturgy, *Sacrosanctum Concilium*, 37.

VI
POSTLUDE

13

PRACTICING HOPE

Francine Cardman

Hope is an elusive virtue, whether theological or practical. It calls us, draw us on, fades into shadow, dies. It bears us up and lets us down. It disappoints and it emboldens. It can be hard to find, harder still to grasp. Theologically, it is, after all, hope *in things unseen* and yet to come. Practically, it is hope that things seen to be awry, unjust, life-threatening can be transformed through a vision of what could be possible now. At times, the elusiveness of hope is due to mistaking one kind of hope for the other. At other times, it is felt in the collision of our own limited abilities with the seeming intractability of powerfully arrayed interests. How do we sustain hope in the face of setbacks, failure, painfully slow progress, or a timeline that might well extend beyond our own lifetime?

The immediate context of this reflection on practicing hope is the continued unfolding of the sexual abuse crisis in the Catholic Church and the efforts to support survivors, confront perpetrators and enablers, and reform and heal the Church itself. The Church cannot offer a credible message of hope and salvation to the world if it is unwilling or unable to heal itself in matters so fundamental to its life. The issue of sexual abuse and the integrity of the Church is critical in its own right. But it also presents a paradigm of abusive authority, destructive relationships, and resistance to change that we can see repeated in many other contexts and institutions, whether personal, political, economic, or ecological. The need for justice and healing is urgent in all these contexts; the need for hope in order to remain in the struggle, even more so.

These needs are historical constants. Yet there are moments of crisis (in the root sense of judgment or decision; *krisis* in Greek) and of opportunity (the *opportune* or acceptable time, a turning point; theologically, the day of salvation; *kairos* in Greek), which particularly call us to account for our hope and to commit ourselves to the healing work of justice and love. In so many places and among so many peoples, we are at points of crisis and *kairos* today. Choosing to see the reality before our eyes, judge what is called for, and act opportunely is to engage both history and hope.

Hope and History

Thomas Aquinas reminds us that hope is a virtue oriented to the future, to a difficult but possible good.[1] But it is learned in the present. As a theological virtue, hope is—first and finally—the hope for salvation, the fullness of life with God and all God's people. The fulfillment of hope is also its end, its consummation, when the expected future becomes the endless present. Extending far beyond history, theological hope nevertheless calls us deeper into history, into ourselves, our relationships, and our communities. For it is there, in the discipline of the daily, that hope must be enacted again and again, often in face of all evidence to the contrary. In the ordinariness and perversity of history, we learn and nurture the practice of hope.

These two kinds of hope—theological and practical, eschatological and everyday—are related, for Christians, necessarily so. The great hope for wholeness, for final salvation, is the context for the hope we have for healing in history, for salvation that we begin to glimpse now in part and look forward to in fullness. Both kinds of hope pertain to bodies and souls, persons and institutions, the community of life itself. Practical hope is a reflection of that larger hope, a way of *making seen*, however imperfectly, a future good that is difficult to attain but, to some extent, within our reach now. Practical hope is not optimism, nor is its alternative pessimism. Rather, it is a particular kind of realism, grounded in the possible, tutored by the actual and by failure. Its challenge is to learn from experience how to "keep on keeping on." Attending to practical hope does not detract from theological hope but deepens it. In turn, theological hope can, and for many people does, undergird practical hope. One way of thinking about everyday, practical hope and its relation to theological hope is to understand it as hope for the future of love in history.

Practices and Perspectives

There are no easy answers to the question of how to sustain hope over the long haul, in discouraging conditions, in face of loss and failure. For the most part, I am posing this question and suggesting some possible ways of supporting everyday hope in regard to matters of social or structural change—situations of injustice, wrongdoing, suffering, and of resistance to the change required to ameliorate them. To some extent, the suggestions offered here might also address the kind of practical hope needed to sustain oneself in ministry or direct service with those who suffer from these injustices or from illness and other forms of loss. I do not assume, however, that these practices necessarily speak to personal suffering in body or spirit and the hope necessary to endure it, though there may be ways in which they relate to such experiences as well.

What practices and perspectives might help us maintain balance and direction, reaffirm vision, replenish energy, and sustain hope in situations of injustice and struggle? Those I suggest here—proprioception, passion, power, and persistence—may vary in their aptness according to persons and circumstances; they may prove helpful for some but not for others. Yet attending to these practices may be generative of additional ones while also increasing the range of resources available to all of us who are in need of hope in hard times.

Proprioception

"Proprioception," meaning (at root) self-perception or self-awareness, is a term from physiology. In its first sense, proprioception is a natural process of biofeedback by which the body "knows" where it is, especially where its limbs are and how to move them in order to get from one place to another. It is a perception of the physical self in time and space and motion that is essential to animal and, therefore, human life. On a metaphorical level, proprioception, as a practice of hope, can help us to know where we are, what we are feeling, where we want to go, and how to move from here to there.

In this second sense, proprioception is an intentional and self-reflexive process. Its aim is to attend to feeling, listen to the self, and bring this inner dialogue to external expression. There are many mediums through which to engage in this process: proprioceptive writing, "painting from the source," and focusing are ready examples.[2] The self-awareness these practices elicit is a means of orienting ourselves to the world by integrating body, feeling, thought, and action. Especially in times of disorientation and distress, knowing what our deepest feelings are can help us find ourselves, know where we are, where we want to be, and how to get there. Engaging in this kind of proprioception can become a spiritual discipline that integrates everyday hope and action for justice. By connecting us to ourselves, practices of proprioception enable us to move toward what we desire. Moving forward (again, or for the first time) opens us to others on the same path, thereby creating small but significant movements of hope.

Passion

In its root meaning, passion is feeling that moves us. It is an experience of being affected by or subject to something, of suffering in the sense of allowing the feeling and its source to touch and change us. Passion is feeling that is consonant with our deepest self. It draws us outside of ourselves and reaches toward the feelings and desires of others. In relation to hope, passion manifests itself in patience (or suffering) and, perhaps less obviously, in pleasure.

Patience is an experience of being susceptible, of undergoing, of suffering, of enduring—hence also of waiting. It requires a kind of groundedness that is willing to make space for the unwelcome and unwanted, yet without letting go of the hope for what it desires to see take their place. Patience refuses to let the absence of what it seeks close down the horizon of possibility. Looked at from another viewpoint, patience stands against the tide of despair. The waiting that patience endures is not passive, but active. It is expectation, not resignation. Patience is a passion for the good combined with the courage to keep watch and to work for its presence.

Pleasure, too, is a passion, a feeling that moves us from within and without. It is joy in the moment, delight in the immediate—the material. But it is also joy in the evanescent; that which does not last, and in hints of something more; that which is not yet. Pleasure is physical and spiritual, the play of spirit and matter, time and eternity. And sometimes it is just *play*—play that is simple exuberance, play that recreates at the most basic levels. Pleasure, too, has its own kind of suffering in the experience of its limits and absence. Recognizing this link prevents us from sundering patience and pleasure as if they were antithetical to each other. Pleasure is a form of passion that makes patience and, therefore, hope, possible.

Learning to live and act from passion opens us to *compassion*, sharing in the passion of others, responding to their need for hope and desire for healing, the actions they take for themselves and for their communities. This compassionate sharing is already a movement of hope in the face of hardship. Passion and compassion join us to each other through patience and the simple pleasure of working together toward a difficult but attainable good, not only for ourselves, but also for others and for the world.

Power

To connect with our own and others' deep passion is a way to realize and increase the personal and communal power needed to sustain everyday hope. This is power with and for, not power over. It is a resource that expands with use and can neither be exhausted nor hoarded. Power of this sort is renewable—and also renews its users—because it is the power of human spirit and Holy Spirit, the synergy of community and communion. In ways consonant with our histories and commitments (and sometimes quite unexpectedly), we touch and are touched by the power of spirit/Spirit not only through acting together, but through prayer and meditation, prophecy and vision, and through poetry.

Prayer, in its multivalent expressions, opens us to the power of spirit/Spirit while also allowing us to lament its absence or loss. As praise, thanksgiving, petition, lament, confession, protest, grief, rage, rejoicing, silence, listening, centering, letting go, or holding on, prayer is an act of hope, making a space for itself— even in the face of hopelessness. For Christians, prayer and meditation centered on Jesus' life, death, and resurrection are a way to place historical realities into the larger context of theological hope and return to the dailiness of struggle with renewed commitment. Whether discursive or silent, iconic or imageless, ritualized or spontaneous, solitary or communal, prayer and meditation can ground and draw us together, strengthen our hearts, and empower us to enter or reenter a dialogue of hope.

Prophecy and vision (whether experienced directly through oneself, made known through ancient or contemporary accounts of encounters with spirit/Spirit, or through the shared prophecy that is the fruit of communal prayer and vision) challenge our assumptions, chastise presumption, and call us to clarity and action. Vision and prophecy draw us beyond ourselves to a power that both is and is not our own, sight that exceeds imagination, words and works that surpass ability—and sometimes fail in their purpose. Often these are words of consolation, works of mercy, visions of healing and restoration, seen and heard in a great compassion that can, paradoxically, border on outrage. Prophecy and vision enacted in words and deeds cry out against evil and injustice, demanding repentance and redress, promising life and wholeness if we turn from the ways of death. No easy path, but a fierce tenderness marks its hope and opens the way before us.

Poetry, too, is a way to draw on and deepen the spirit/Spirit of our personal and communal power. Poetry is flesh made word, the spirit of truth, the revelation of experience. Writing or reading poetry can help us find the clarity to see the world and ourselves and know what needs to be done. It can evoke pathos and terror, courage and hope, the stillness at the heart of things. Like prophecy and vision, poetry challenges and consoles in its outrage and tenderness. "Poetry," as Audre Lorde insists, "is not a luxury." Rather, "It forms the quality of the light within which we predicate our hopes and dreams toward survival and change, first made into language, then into an idea, then into more tangible action."[3] Whether we identify as political, spiritual, or both, we need the light and life force of poetry in order to make our way toward hope and healing.

Prayer, prophecy and vision, and poetry are practices that offer us gifts of insight and hope, consolation and challenge, realism about the present and the possible, desire for what might yet be, the power to carry on.

Persistence

Persistence in the movement toward a difficult good is itself an act of hope. We exercise persistence through presence and through protest. *Presence* has many manifestations: simply being there and being with, in the moment or over many moments; bearing witness to another's truths; standing in solidarity with those who suffer injustice and others who, with them, seek its transformation. Our ability to stay present to others is mutually

221

dependent on our ability to stay present to ourselves. In terms of practicing hope, whether personally or communally, persistent presence is a persuasive witness that goes beyond argument to strike a much deeper chord in persons and, often unexpectedly, institutions. Such presence is a quiet call to hope, engendering action that makes change possible.

Sometimes persistence requires more visible and vocal expression in public *protest*. Resistance—whether in writing or speech, standing or marching, through ritual or street theater, by keeping vigil—enacts hope among participants, evokes hope among at least some observers, and calls us all to accountability. As practices of hope, protest and resistance can arise from the power of anger (at injustice, the rupturing of relationship, the violation of ideals) that moves us to do the work of love (seeking justice, righting relationships, restoring integrity).[4] Here it is important to be clear that anger is a source of information, not a mode of action. Doing the truth in love requires constant self-examination and openness to dialogue in order to prevent persistence from devolving into mere stubbornness. Protest is a means to a difficult good, not an end in itself. At moments of crisis and *kairos*, it becomes a necessity.

Persistence is a gift of the human spirit, cultivated interiorly and also in the community of kindred spirits seeking justice as the form of love. It is hope making its way slowly but steadfastly through history.[5]

Hope for Healing

Crises abound throughout this country and across the world: the plundering of natural resources and the ecological destruction that accompanies it; nearly constant streams of refugees fleeing seemingly endless conflicts; rape as an evermore widely used weapon of war; the global reach of economic destabilization; only the beginning of a depressingly long list that is all too easy to construct. Yet in these crises are also moments of *kairos*, the opportunity to make change for the better, to choose healing rather than the perpetuation of harm, communion rather than narrow personal and corporate self-interest.

Practicing hope does not guarantee that we will succeed in reaching the good we desire. We live in finitude, short of perfection. All our efforts have their limits, even our efforts at hope. To abandon practical hope, however, is to abandon ourselves and history, the world and God, whatever we know as the ground of being, life itself. Daring to act in hope requires that we acknowledge imperfection and accept that even our best efforts can and, with some regularity, will be defeated. At those times, we need not only the practices of hope suggested here (and many others), but a shift in perspective. We need to take a longer view of time and history. We need the perspective of a paleontologist[6] or astrophysicist, for instance; a process philosopher or theologian.

Within that longer view, the practices of everyday hope flow into each other in ways that begin to shape a shared perspective on history, hope, and healing. They ask that we take time, look and listen inward, attend to deep feeling. They ask that we cultivate both patience and pleasure, presence and protest. They seek the power of spirit/Spirit deep within ourselves and in the synergy of hope shared among a few or many. Each of these practices has an inward movement and an outward energy. They move toward hope and healing in our own lives and, at the same time, reach out to other lives and communities. Each of these practices is grounded in the present, the real, the material, and draws on the power of spirit/Spirit to enflesh the future of love in history.

The ongoing crisis of sexual abuse in the Catholic Church is only one moment of *kairos*. But if, in this moment, we learn to sustain hope through practices of proprioception, passion, power of spirit/Spirit, and persistence; if we continue to work toward healing the church, then that learning will be available for us to draw on and share in other contexts. If we live the connection between everyday hope and theological hope, we can begin to touch the larger need for healing in the world.[7] For in the end, commitment to hope and healing in the Church is not for the Church itself, but for the world—for the human community and for the whole community of life on earth.

Notes

1. Thomas Aquinas, *Summa Theologiae*, vol. 21 (Ia2ae. 40-48), *Fear and Anger* (New York: Cambridge University Press, 2006), quest. 40, art. 5, response.

2. For proprioceptive writing, see Linda Trichter Metcalf and Simon Tobin, *Writing the Mind Alive: The Proprioceptive Method for Finding Your Authentic Voice* (New York: Random House, 2002) and the website of the PW Center, http://www.pwriting.org/ (accessed July 4, 2011).

For painting, see Aviva Gold and Elena Oumano, Painting from the Source: Awakening the Artist's Soul in Everyone (New York: HarperCollins, 1998; reprint, Source Publications) and the website, http://paintingfromthesource.com/ (accessed July 4, 2011).

For focusing, see Eugene T. Gendlin, Focusing (New York: BantamDell, 1978, 1981) and the website, http://www.focusing.org/index.html (accessed July 4, 2011).

3. Audre Lorde, "Poetry is Not a Luxury," in *Sister Outsider: Essays and Speeches* (Trumansburg, NY: Crossing Press, 1984), 37.

4. See Beverly Harrison's now classic essay, "The Power of Anger in the Work of Love: Christian Ethics for Women and Other Strangers," in *Making the Connections: Essays in Feminist Social Ethics*, ed. Carol S. Robb, 1–21 (Boston: Beacon Press, 1985).

5. In speeches and sermons, Martin Luther King, Jr. frequently made use of an image he had paraphrased from Theodore Parker, a nineteenth-century Unitarian minister and abolitionist. "The arc of the moral universe is long," King would say, "but it bends toward justice." He used it in one of his late speeches (1967), in which he memorably explicated the relationship of power, love, and justice: "Power at its best is love implementing the demands of justice, and justice at its best is power correcting everything that stands against love." See "Where Do We Go From Here?" in A Testament of Hope: The Essential Writings and Speeches

of Martin Luther King Jr., ed. James M. Washington (New York: HarperCollins, 1986), 253, 247. King was assassinated in April 1968.

6. The Jesuit priest, paleontologist, and theologian, Teilhard de Chardin, observed—in regard to human progress and change in history—that it was necessary to take the viewpoint of a paleontologist; and that human advancement would require "a great hope held in common." See "Some Reflections on Progress," in *Future of Man*, trans. Norman Denny, 61–72 (New York, Harper & Row, 1964), quotation at 72.

7. Some resources for further reflection on hope include: Flora A. Keshgegian, *Time for Hope: Practices for Living in Today's World* (New York: Continuum, 2006); Margaret Farley, "Feminism and Hope," in *Full of Hope: Critical Social Perspectives on Theology*, ed. Magdala Thompson, 20–40 (New York: Paulist Press, 2003); Dermot A. Lane, *Keeping Hope Alive: Stirrings in Christian Theology* (New York: Paulist Press, 1996); Paul G. Crowley, *Unwanted Wisdom: Suffering, the Cross, and Hope* (New York: Continuum, 2005). The latter addresses personal suffering.

ABOUT THE AUTHORS

Francine Cardman is Associate Professor of Historical Theology and Church History at the Boston College School of Theology and Ministry. She is a past president of the North American Academy of Ecumenists and has served on the Eastern Orthodox/Roman Catholic Consultation in the United States.

M. Shawn Copeland is Associate Professor of Theology at Boston College and a former president (2003–2004) of the Catholic Theological Society of America. She is the author of over 100 articles, reviews, and book chapters, among which is *The Subversive Power of Love: The Vision of Henriette Delille* (Paulist Press, 2009).

Frank Desiderio, CSP, is a member of the Paulist Fathers. He has worked as a parish priest, campus minister, seminary rector, and producer of film, TV, and radio; he strives to connect people with the experience of a loving God in mediums both secular and sacred. Currently, he is director of the Paulist Center in downtown Boston.

Kate Dooley, OP, has published widely in catechetical and liturgical journals and written a number of texts and resources for catechesis with a particular focus on liturgical catechesis.

Peter E. Fink, SJ, is Professor Emeritus from the former Weston Jesuit School of Theology (Cambridge, MA) and is currently Associate Pastor at St. Francis Xavier Church (NYC). Among his publications are: *Worship: Praying the Sacraments; New Dictionary of Sacramental Worship* (editor), and *Alternative Futures of Worship* (editor, *Reconciliation and Anointing*).

Raymond G. Helmick, SJ, is Professor of Conflict Resolution at Boston College. He served as unofficial emissary between Catholic and Protestant paramilitary groups in Ulster and is a founder of the U.S. Interreligious Committee for Peace in the Middle East. He is the author of *Living Catholic Faith in a Contentious Age* (Continuum, 2010).

Thomas A. Kane, CSP, a Paulist priest, teaches at the Boston College School of Theology and Ministry. He is the Director of Paulist Reconciliation Ministries, Washington, DC. He has recently edited the new *Landings* program (Paulist Press) with Anna LaNave, which welcomes returning Catholics. As a liturgical videographer, his video collection, *The Dancing Church around the World* (Paulist Press), has been shown internationally.

Melissa M. Kelley is associate professor of pastoral care and contextual education at Boston College.

Michael McGarry, CSP, a Paulist priest, has served at the University of Texas, Boston's Paulist Center, St. Paul's College (Washington, DC) and at the University of California at Berkeley. With a specialty in Jewish–Christian relations, for eleven years, he was Rector of the Tantur Ecumenical Institute in Jerusalem. Since 2010, he serves as president for the Paulist Fathers in Queens, NY. He is author of *Christology after Auschwitz*, and co-author of *Pope John Paul II in the Holy Land* and *Pope Benedict XVI in the Holy Land* (all Paulist Press).

Hosffman Ospino, PhD, is Assistant Professor of Pastoral Theology and Religious Education at Boston College's School of Theology and Ministry (STM), where he is also the Director of the university's graduate programs in Hispanic Ministry. He is the editor of *Hispanic Ministry in the Twenty-First Century: Present and Future* (Convivium Press, 2010) and the author of *Peter's Catechism: Who Do You Say That I Am? Why Did You Doubt? Do You Love Me?* (Liguori, 2011).

Rodney L. Petersen is Executive Director of the Boston Theological Institute and teaches courses on the issues of religion and conflict in the Institute's member schools. He is an ordained minister in the Presbyterian Church, U.S.A., and among his publications are the following: co-editor of *Forgiveness and Reconciliation: Religion, Public Policy, and Conflict Transformation* (Templeton Foundation Press, 2002) and *Formation for Life: Just Peacemaking and 21st Century Discipleship* (Wipf and Stock Publishers, 2012).

Thomas W. Porter is a trial lawyer, mediator, teacher, and minister. He teaches at Boston University School of Theology, where he directs a concentration in Religion and Conflict Transformation, and he is the Co-Executive Director of JUST-PEACE Center for Mediation and Conflict Transformation in The United Methodist Church. He is the editor of the book, *Conflict and Communion: Reconciliation and Restorative Justice at Christ's Table*, the author of *The Spirit and Art of Conflict Transformation: Creating a Culture of JustPeace*, and co-author of *The Journey: Forgiveness, Restorative Justice and Reconciliation*.

Thomas P. Ryan, CSP, served as Director of the Canadian Centre for Ecumenism (1981–1995), Co-founder and Director of Unitas, an ecumenical center for spirituality in Montreal, QC (1995–2000), and Founder–director of the Paulist North American Office for Ecumenical and Interfaith Relations in Washington, DC (2000 to present). He has authored or co-authored 14 books, 150 articles in journals and periodicals, and offers a monthly article to interested church newspapers. www.tomryancsp.org.

Thomas Stegman, SJ, is Associate Professor of New Testament at the Boston College School of Theology and Ministry. A member of the Wisconsin Province of the Society of Jesus, he is author of *The Character of Jesus: The Linchpin to Paul's Argument in 2 Corinthians* (Pontifical Biblical Press) and *Second Corinthians* (Baker Academic).

Robert J. Schreiter, CPPS, is Vatican Council II Professor of Theology at Catholic Theological Union in Chicago. He is the author of *Reconciliation: Mission and Ministry in a Changing Social Order* and *The Ministry of Reconciliation: Spirituality and Strategies*.